With a Song in My Psyche

With a Song in My Psyche

On the Psychology of Singing and
Teaching Singing

Pearl Shinn Wormhoudt

To order additional copies of this book, contact:
Xlibris Corporation
1-888-7-XLIBRIS
www.Xlibris.com
Orders@Xlibris.com

TO THE MEMORY OF
MY DEAR AND GREAT TEACHER

DONNA PAOLA NOVIKOVA

Contents

ACKNOWLEDGEMENTS

This book is the result of a lifetime of work and play and study along the four lines that make a voice teacher. I have great debts to acknowledge in all four lines.

I owe to Paola Novikova and her study with Mattia Battistini the understanding of the Italian bel canto tradition. This understanding is not only an intellectual one, but one she helped me work out in my own voice.

In the area of body management and release into expression, I owe Hanya Holm and Alvin Nikolais for modern dance training in expressive movement. I owe John Stitely for teaching me the short form of Tai Chi. Special thanks are due to Joan Murray, Jane Heirich, and Mary Montgomery for their patient teaching of the Alexander Technique. I owe Joseph Gifford for his teaching of Trager Mentastics, which I in turn teach all my students.

My debts are many to those who helped me understand voice science and the psychology of incorporating that knowledge in my teaching. First was William Vennard with whom I discussed vocal registers. One of my greatest debts is to Berton Coffin for his work in vowel acoustics, and for his leading me to Mme. Novikova. Finally, I have learned about the vocal instrument from Ingo Titze and Johan Sundberg, as well as from many voice scientists in the Care of the Professional Voice Symposia at Juilliard and then in Philadelphia.

In the fourth area, gaining an understanding of a singer's psychology, I owe all my teachers and all my students. I owe voice teacher colleagues for fruitful discussions, and I greatly owe all the psychologists listed in the bibliography, particularly Kyle Pruett who introduced me to the work of D.W. Winnicott.

In making the book, Jean Thomas, who teaches voice at Iowa State University and sings in Musica Antiqua, helped me untangle long sentences and dangling participles. Robert Edwin, private teacher and "Bach to Rock" columnist for the Journal of Singing, looked at the chapter on the adolescent singer. Paul Kiesgen, chair of the Indiana University Voice Department, and who teaches vocal pedagogy, gave me encouragement. Marvin Keenze, professor of voice and pedagogy at Westminster Choir School, Rider University, advised me about the Tomatis work, and I am grateful for the accuracy of his explanation. Bass Ryan Allen shared his experience as a successful career singer, and Stephanie Samaras, over time, has shared both as a singer and as successful teacher of many Broadway career singers.

For permission to use lengthy quotes from the writing of Victor Fields, and other quotes from The NATS Bulletin and Journal of Singing, I am indebted to William A. Vessels, Executive Director, representing the National Association of Teachers of Singing, Inc.

My student Susan Beckett took over listing the bibliography from my barely readable cards. And, far beyond the call of friendship, Reye Goedeken put together the whole book on her computer.

Finally, I am grateful to my husband, Arthur, to son Joda, and to daughter-in-law Michal Truelsen, for encouragement and critiques over much time. They gave me courage, from their perspective as early music singers. My deepest debt of all is to Arthur, whose devotion to developing his theory of literature has been a constant example and inspiration.

L'Invitation au Voyage (Duparc)

INTRODUCTION

This book is written for singers and teachers of singers. A singer, at whatever level of performance, can be a blessing to his community, be it local or worldwide, expressing its joys and sorrows, its concerns and needs, its deepest thoughts and feelings. A knowledgeable and caring teacher is a blessing to singers and their communities, for we never know where a seed sown will bring a musical harvest.

Good singing is based on technique and artistry. Both of these abilities are based on the singer's physiology, physics and psychology. Great singing is attained with fuller engagement of psychological dynamics underlying both technique and artistry. As singers and teachers of singers we have come a long way in the last fifty years in attaining and organizing the information needed to build a solid technique. Much of what was a mystery is no longer so. In our modern fast-paced world this new clarity of how to attain healthy expressive vocal sound is much needed. Vocal pedagogy programs can now combine the best of the old intuitive training with the present scientifically-based understanding of the instrument.

It is my thesis that we need to do more of this same clarifying work to understand and make use of the underlying psychological truths of song-making. This is greatly needed by singers who want to make it a life's work. It is also needed by our society, by whom artists of all kinds are thought to be "different" and special, but not terribly necessary.

The problem is that they are terribly necessary—all of them, singers, dancers, painters, composers, instrumentalists, writers, actors. Modern Western society is strong on conquering the outer world, as witness the bursts of technological inventions. Humanity needs to understand and control the inner world, the thoughts, emotions and beliefs that energize either constructive or destructive activities. This is what we sing about, in many metaphors and circumstances.

Somewhere in this dense experience and daily self formation there sometimes grows a singer, or a teacher of singing. In this book I will try to pull out the psychological threads upon which these musicians function. My main subject is the psychology of the singer. If we can clarify that, then what the teacher of singers needs to be, needs to know, needs to do will also be implied and clarified.

Once, singers and voice teachers were afraid of knowing too much about the physics and physiology of the vocal instrument. In the last couple of decades voice teachers and voice scientists have become acquainted, and their new sharing and the new technologies have enlightened us a great deal on the elements of vocal technique and how to better pursue vocal development and therapy. Physicist Richard Feynman says: "Poets say science takes away from the beauty of the stars—mere globs of imagination—stuck on this carousel my eye can catch eighteen-billion-year-old light. It does no harm to the mystery to know a little about it".

Are we now to be afraid of knowing too much of the underlying reasons for singing the feelings we "interpret", that is, afraid of knowing too much about the psychology?

Of the 3-P's mentioned above, we have paid the least attention to psychological factors, so that on an everyday basis we know a great deal about them, but our knowledge is scattered, intuitive. What we recognize as artistry stems from all three, so as a profession we need more understanding of the singer's psychological gifts, of what stands in the way of their use, and how they can be strengthened.

I am reminded of the story of the little girl who was asked to play some Chopin for a great pianist. When she finished, the pianist said, "Well, that's fine playing, but rather odd Chopin". "You see", said the little girl, "first I learn the notes, then the expression, and finally I put in the sharps and flats, but I haven't got that far with this piece yet". Perhaps there is a need in a singer's psyche for some sharpening and flattening!

Indeed, we know a great deal about ourselves as singers and teachers of singers, but some of this has not been written, and some has been seen only in parts. This book is an attempt to put some of these parts together, so we may begin to see a bigger picture of the singer's psychological dynamics. Technique will wander into the discussion when it affects or is affected by the psychology in the situation, but this book's contribution to better singing fundamentally resides in the domains of nature/nurture and of body/mind.

Both singers and teachers get so bound up in the technical problems encountered that it is easy to overlook or not find time to consider the underlying psychology. But state of mind can affect the breathing, affect control of the support system, cause interfering muscle tensions, diminish courage to make brave sounds, undermine trust of the teacher and of self's ability, wipe out verbal or musical memories, cause fears of not being perfect on high notes or low notes or on pitches or on everything, and finally, can elevate performance anxiety. Of course, using psychological strengths brings just the opposite desirable results.

Beyond gaining a correct, healthy (therefore beautiful) technique, the singer has four more tasks which demand that his psyche work with his brain, as well as with his physics and physiology. The first of these is gaining self-confidence, so that he trusts his instrument and his abilities. Secondly, he must develop a stage presence. He has inherited his body shape and functioning, but his self-image controls the impact of his performance. With this realistic and accepted image of body and mind, the third task is to gain a sense of flow, a new creative expressiveness. This leads finally to the great task, which is artistry.

Far from detracting from our art, clearer knowledge contributes to better voice building and vocal health. If we can gain more knowledge of the psychological roots of singing, what a boon it can be to the whole demanding process!

In this process, fully realized, the singer not only discovers his true voice, but his true self. The correct healthy technique allows self-acceptance of his voice, self-confidence in giving, a calm body and a concentrated mind, emotional expression, devotion to the music and poetry, good health and energy.

I believe it is not generally recognized how tender is the performing self, or the student's "heart" in the one-on-one voice lesson. The tennis star John McEnroe said, "It's difficult when you're out there on the court. You're really exposing your whole soul". If this is true for someone who just needs to hit a ball with a racket, how far more true for someone to let go of sounds that reveal his innermost thoughts and feelings.

We need first of all to look at the roots of the singing behavior. The deepest roots are two-fold: the nature of the musical brain, and the development of early childhood language, song, and as we musicians insist, play. This early growth is fueled with strong emotions.

Having these two roots in mind will then allow us to consider the mind/body give-and-take. We will look at body activities such as breathing, movement, and body language, and at the mind/body correlation of senses, feelings, expressiveness, self-image, and identity as a singer and as a person.

Since the majority of learning singers are in their teens or early twenties, we must then understand the special situation of the adolescent singer who is trying to gain both his identity and emotional control. We then can look at whatever influences gender factors may have. This may be more important for singers than for instrumental musicians. Certainly both are capable, emotional, and expressive, but pianos and clarinets are the same for both boys and girls. Not quite true of the vocal instrument, nor of the psyche that initiates the sound of that instrument.

With all this background in mind, we will look at the moment, to see, for instance, what brings on the common problem of performance anxiety, linked as it is to standards of perfection. If we understand these anxieties, these inhibitions, we are empowered to intentionally facilitate the needed body/mind interactions. The resulting poised balance in lessons, in rehearsals, in performance is one of self-confidence, awareness, concentration, creativity. This is possible for both the amateur and the professional singer.

At that point we will look at the realities of the professional singer's life. When a singer in the middle of his studies begins to dream of this career, he and his teacher need to look at those realities, to judge whether he has not only the talent but the temperament for that life, and whether that is truly the best way to invest his talent.

Singing and teaching singing have been my lifetime love and work and play, so I cannot explore the singer's psyche impersonally. I will have to move from general statements to "I" and "they" experience, and to "you" suggestions. My observations have occurred through eight years of social work, ten years of voice lessons and coaching, then more than forty years of teaching voice and vocal pedagogy, and giving faculty recitals. I also draw on several schools of psychological thought where the point of view can enlighten our experience as singers. I have made preliminary studies and observations in three papers given at international conferences of voice teachers or of music psychologists, in Rotterdam, Philadelphia, and the University of Liège, Belgium. I must say as did an anonymous sage, "*I have drunk from wells I did not dig—I have been warmed by fires I did not build*".

I take heart from what John F. Kennedy once said: "The poet, the artist, the musician, continues the quiet work of the centuries, building bridges of experience between people, reminding man of the universality of his feelings and desires and despairs".

This book is a first step, and it is my hope that singers, teachers, and psychologists can build on this framework. Knowledge frees us, expressing deep meanings frees us, to integrate our self and our song and contribute to liberation in our society.

The invitation to the voyage is made. Let us embark.

> Are not religion, love and music three expressions of one and the same situation, the need for extending the self which stirs in every noble spirit?
>
> —Honoré de Balzac

CHAPTER I

Where the Music Comes From (Lee Hoiby)

THE MUSICAL BRAIN

There is one question which underlies this entire book: Why do we sing? Our brain has stored up the how and the why of our singing, and that is where we must begin.

The brain runs the show. Everyone can benefit from knowing something about his/her brain, how it is constructed and how it works. The singer, the performer, can certainly feel more secure when he knows he can depend on his awesome brain to pull together all the technical messages sent to his vocal instrument (his body), combined with all his feelings for both the poetry and the music, combined with whatever mastery is needed of the environment to allow the performance. The brain runs the whole show.

A singer does not need to know detailed neuroanatomy but it helps to know he has ten billion or more neurons at his command for the work. Somewhere in the singer's head lies the motivation to make a sound. When that happens the trained brain-nervous system must simultaneously or in quick sequence send out these orders:

—cope with any excess performance anxiety,
—check correct body position,
—keep up the subconscious beating of the heart to deliver oxygen to the brain to keep its instructions clear, and to deliver glucose to muscles to energize their working,

—position the larynx to leave the vocal folds free to vibrate, and instruct adjacent muscles such as those in tongue and jaw not to interfere,

—remember the vowels, and instruct muscles in pharynx, tongue, soft palate, jaw, lips to form the vowels clearly and with resonance, but not in an over-productive way,

—have some feelings for the unconscious non-verbal meaning of the music of the song, and relate the vowel timbre to that meaning,

—manage the breath on onset of sound and continuation of the phrase,

—maintain the chemical balance which keeps producing saliva to mouth and larynges otherwise too dry to produce sound,

—remember the already discovered meaning of the poetic text of the song so as to carry out the performance plan,

—remember the pitches,

—remember the rhythm,

—articulate the consonants,

—control dynamic levels,

—call up memories of the relevant emotions and experiences that will add nuances to the expression of meaning.

This is some of what the musical brain has to put together. On paper it looks like a formidable task, if not impossible. But with careful thought and training it is not only possible, it is easy. So psychologically we have the situation in which a young person decides to take voice lessons in order to sing better. He may think this will consist chiefly of singing songs, learning new songs, and having the teacher tell him how to sing the songs. He may have little idea of what a great adventure he is beginning, to gain an ever-clearer mental concept of healthy sound production and ever-increasing expressiveness of the meaning of the music and the poem. Through this adventure he recognizes his true voice and finds a large part of his true self.

Here we come to the point that the voice teacher must forever keep in mind. Victor A. Fields wrote an on-the-mark article on this: *How Mind Governs Voice*. His basic message is that the teacher must always simultaneously further both the student's development of an habitual correct technique, and of a competence to think, act, interpret, and express musically. This is the student's exciting work. This is the teacher's challenge, opening channels for the student's discovery and success. Fields says, "A primary objective is to develop the *mental* faculties that control singing". William Vennard said: "We do not teach singing, we teach singers".

Fields describes four basic psychological factors that enter into the cultivation of the artist singer's voice: "First, that mental imagery governs voice control; Second, that the singer's art is a product of habit formation; Third, that self-expression is a basic human instinct; and Fourth, that singing is essentially an expression of enthusiasm or joy in life".

The first two parallel my thinking that the mental concept must continually become clearer, and that correct habits are formed by never *practicing* a wrong production. I cannot state the last two factors in any better way. On practicing there is a story about Lauritz Melchior, that he practiced a mistake so well he never forgot it. Ideally, the teacher helps the student unblock external physical hindrances or internal emotional restraints. This is the mind/body work. This allows the voice to be free.

Fields further points out that man is not a body containing a mind, but is a mind expressing through the body. "Voice is not merely a mechanism of the body producing a tone. It is tonal image projecting itself through physical channels into audibility. Understanding the basic difference between these two concepts is paramount in vocal teaching. The former is mechanistic, the latter artistic or creative. Therefore, if the tonal image is properly motivated expression will be full of meaning and purpose".

Technical virtuosity does not guarantee artistic singing. Fields again: " . . . bel canto masters pronounced the dictum that there is no singing without saying: that technique and expression are inseparable, and that it is necessary to teach them side by side from the start, . . . to develop a singing personality".

If this is true, we must pose the question, is it beneficial for singers to know anything about how their brains work? How the brain enables them to be the singer they want to be? They certainly benefit from knowing something about the physics and physiology of the vocal instrument, for then they can work with the natural functioning, not against it. The same is true of knowing what we do know about how the brain works.

When the singer knows how magnificent is his brain, he can be confident that it will support his ability to sing. He can be assured of the richness of memories, experiences, and understanding that gives deep meaning to his singing and his song. He can develop his singing personality.

Remember what John McEnroe said about a performer revealing his soul. We have a strong identification with our speech. Words/sounds are what "my mind" thinks, what "my heart" feels, what "my imagination" dreams. We reveal all this in the words/ sounds we make, even when we speak of prosaic everyday matters. A greater revelation is possible when we dramatically raise this word/sound into song.

Bernice Johnson Reagon, emerita curator of the Smithsonian Institute National Museum of American History and founder of the vocal group *Sweet Honey in the Rock*, says "I find that when I'm singing I always know who and where I am". And Rainer Maria Rilke puts it briefly: "To sing is to be".

Sound is a core part of ourselves, and to say it or sing it makes us vulnerable. How will our world receive our thoughts, our emotions, our imaginings? It may be that our vulnerability will lessen and our ability to communicate will increase, if we understand something of our need and our society's need for this sound expression.

In this book we study the psychological principles of how the amazing mind/body we have can make sound production optimal. Since our hugely complex brains run the whole show, it will help if we understand something of how it is constructed and how it functions.

Some researchers are asking the heavy questions: What is music? What does it mean for a human being to be musical? What parts of the brain process music? What happens when we listen to music? The work of Gerald W. Edelman deserves to be followed. He is working on the basic question of how all the diverse sources of a given message are put together. He calls his theory neuronal group selection, about the process of this complex integrating ability.

Until recently, the workings of the brain were a secret. Now discoveries in molecular biology and new imaging technologies reveal some of the workings. We know the messages are electrical and chemical. We do not yet know how the vocal muscles read this message, when for example the larynges set perfectly to sound A220, or A440, or A880! This is a marvel and a mystery in which the singer can take pride. His brain sends the command, his body (instrument) executes it!

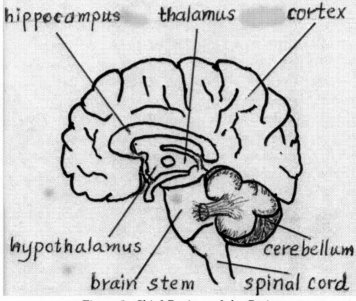

Figure 1: Chief Regions of the Brain

Let us now look at the anatomy of this brain that runs our lives and our performances. The whole brain, the size of a grapefruit or a cabbage, weighs three pounds and has ten billion neurons, each one of which can connect with a thousand others. Growing out of the spinal cord like the crown of a tree out of the trunk, the brain has several major components.

The brain stem, at the top of the spinal cord, helps regulate body states, temperatures, heart rate, and breathing. It also monitors and filters all the information coming in through the senses.

The cerebellum, about the size of a fist, is attached to the rear of the brain stem. It controls muscular movements, coordinates them, and adjusts posture. Nearly 90% is set aside to control hands and fingers! It has fine control of the vocal mechanism.

Only recently have new data been gathered on the cerebellum, which shows that it does much more than regulate movement. There is a large information highway feeding messages out from the cerebral cortex to the cerebellum through the pons. Processed data is fed back from the cerebellum to the cerebral cortex via the thalamus. The information sequence then is: cerebral cortex—pons—cerebellum—thalamus-cortex.

New imaging techniques allowed researchers to see that the cerebellum is involved with higher thought. Jonathan Leonard reports a new theory: that the cerebellum not only regulates the rate, force, rhythm and accuracy of movement, but also regulates the speed, capacity, consistency and appropriateness of thought—in short, that the cerebellum's business is to detect, predict, and correct errors involving movement, perception, memory, thought, or a mixture of these. It probably helps turn our thoughts into words, to pin down part of what we are thinking.

Certainly a singer's cerebellum is working hard for him. It seems likely that it has a role in identifying objects by touch, exercising conscious thought, generating words, processing music and other sounds, mentally rotating abstract objects, influencing emotions such as sadness, depression, fear, learning repetitive skills such as singing on key and storing the information needed to exercise these skills.

On the top of the brain stem is the limbic system, which regulates the emotions, and which includes the amygdala, part of the thalamus, the hypothalamus, and the hippocampus. We use the hippocampus to form long-term memories, to retrieve old ones, and to manage explicit, conscious memory.

The pituitary gland, the master gland of the body, hangs down from the brain stem, and it produces the hormones that govern growth and development. The hypothalamus directs the pituitary gland. The hypothalamus, about the size of a pea, regulates eating, drinking, sleeping, waking, body temperature, balance, and many other functions.

The cerebrum lies over the top of the brain and dominates it. This contains the areas that control thought and consciousness, so that we can remember our past, understand the present, and look to the future. It is divided into two halves, the right and left hemispheres, which are connected by a thick bundle made up of 300 million nerve fibers, called the corpus callosum. Each hemisphere has four lobes: frontal, occipital, parietal, and temporal. The frontal lobe is primarily involved in making plans and decisions, and directing purposeful behavior.

The parietal lobe receives sensory information from the body. Part of the occipital lobe is involved in vision, so sometimes it is called the visual cortex. The temporal lobe manages the important functions of hearing, perception, and language memory, all of which the singer uses extensively.

Covering each hemisphere is a 1/8 inch thick folded layer of nerve cells called the cortex. This is the newest part of the human brain and it first appeared in our ancestors about two hundred million years ago. With it, we remember, communicate, organize, understand, and create. Our most human attribute is speech, and nerves from lips and tongue occupy far more space in the cortex than do those from the entire surface of the torso.

THE TWO HEMISPHERES

At first it was thought that the right and left hemispheres each had specialized functions that were employed quite independently of each other. It is now understood these specialties are often shared and enhanced by both hemispheres. What is not shared is that each hemisphere controls the opposite side of the body.

The left hemisphere deals with language, consonantal sounds, rules of grammar. It has two regions known as Broca's and Wernicke's that mediate language. It classifies objects into standard linguistically defined categories.

The right hemisphere responds to musical characteristics of sound. It has spatial tasks, with fine sensory discriminations, so that it can recognize faces and tactile patterns. Both hemispheres process vowel sounds, and access the meaning of words.

The left hemisphere processes the signals of high visual frequencies which give the details, whereas the right deals with very large low-spatial frequencies of both vision and audition. Therefore the left hemisphere focuses on only one meaning, whereas the right maintains an all-over perception, or an alternate meaning of ambiguous words (jokes, metaphors).

Robert Ornstein states that these large waves form the fundamental background images of our world view, such as the overall sense of our body in space. It is the small waves, like the overtones in sound, that give the precision, the details, and the brilliance.

Ornstein says that auditory processing follows the same lines. Both *in utero* and in a new-born, the right hemisphere receives the low frequency sounds, and the left hemisphere seems to become more highly specialized for handling the high auditory frequencies. It becomes clear that the singer's brain is well able to put all this information together to gain a musical concept.

The corpus callosum connecting the two hemispheres is larger in musicians' brains than in non-musicians. This allows more possibility of communication between the hemispheres, and for singers to link and blend the musical and verbal parts of a song. It is interesting to know that non-musicians hear tones in the left ear, and in the right hemisphere. Musicians reverse this, and hear through the right ear, left hemisphere. Thus, performing high level music comes from the left hemisphere. That is in performance. For musical perception, if the right hemisphere suffers a stroke, perceptual musical ability is lost.

The two hemispheres are specialized in their kind of thought, and kind of emotion. The left produces language, analysis, and makes logical inferences. The right processes information in a non-linear, spatial, synthesizing mode characteristic of music and artistic expression.

They even specialize in emotions, with the left hemisphere involved with feelings of happiness and pleasure, and the right engaged during feelings of anger, disgust, or fear. The fact that the right hemisphere is in control of the large muscles contributes to its negativity, since anger and fear call for large movement, the "fight or flight" response.

Ornstein again: "This doesn't mean that it is all the environment or all the genes, and therefore one hemisphere is all positive or all negative, all thinking or all feeling, or the best way to perceive the world. It is a matter of the way they operate, one handling the larger fundamentals of sound and sight . . . and the other handling the finer distinctions in language, logic, visual detail, and so forth".

As we see, the brain is an amalgam of different structures for different purposes, but because parts communicate with many other parts, the whole is far greater than just the sum of the parts.

NEURONS

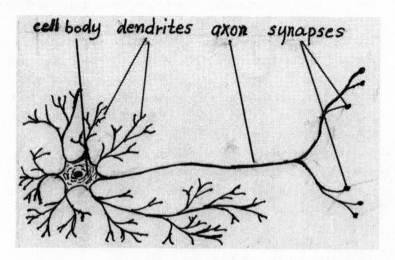

Fig 2: The shape of the neuron

Neurons, or nerve cells, are the building blocks of the brain. No two neurons are identical in form, and brain neurons, in contrast to other body cells, have a unique structure, the synapse. The cell has three regions: the cell body, the dendrites, and the axon. The dendrites are fine tube-like extensions that extend out of the cell body and that branch repeatedly into a tree form. These receive incoming chemical signals which the cell body mediates, sending an electrical message down the axon. The axon may be short or long, so it is possible the message can be carried to far parts of the brain and the nervous system.

The axon then branches into presynaptic terminal fibers which send the communication on to other neurons. The axon does this by converting the electrical message into a chemical one via the neuro-transmitters. These are chemicals which transmit the impulses across a sub-microscopic synaptic space to the receptors on the dendrites of one or many other neurons.

One of these many neurotransmitters is serotonin, which is

special because it does not have receptors located in specific brain areas. Nerve cells deep within the brain stem are tipped with serotonin-sensitive binding sites, and these cells send neuronal tentacles all through the cortical grey matter. So, this uptake and distribution of serotonin affects a great deal of our mental life. Serotonin aids learning and formation of memories. It also enhances the neuron's electrical impulse, which creates enduring memory. Having fewer serotonin-releasing neurons can cause problems such as depression, chronic pain, eating disorders, etc. Drugs such as Prozac and Zoloft seem to aid in the production of more serotonin.

Nerve cells carry out their chemical transitions at great speed. Some of the brain's chemical reactions take as little as one-millionth of a second. As many as 100,000 neurons may be involved in transmitting the information that results in such a simple action as stepping back out of a car's path. All of this takes one second. We can see how it is possible for our brain to manage all the commands needed to sing a song, if we do not place negative thoughts in the way.

CONSCIOUSNESS

The most astonishing capacity of this brain/mind is that we can think about our thinking. We do have memories lodged that are unconscious unless those cells are fired by an electrical probe or are stimulated and released by probing thought. We also have considerable subconscious body activity, in heart, stomach, etc. But, we are conscious of a great deal of brain/mind/body action. This concentrated awareness is most important to the singer.

For example, I began my study with Mme. Paola Novikova in New York at the end of a full semester's sabbatical trip with my husband, through the Middle East and Europe to study music, art, and literature. We returned by boat to have an experience different from flying over the Atlantic. As soon as we reached our hotel I phoned Mme. Novikova, hoping to have a voice lesson yet that afternoon. She said: "You just got off the boat? Go to bed! Rest! You will need all the concentration you can get at tomorrow's lesson". That was true. Even more awareness and concentration are required in performance. For this, we need to learn how to direct our brain/mind's thoughts.

I will not take up the question here of how it is that we have this consciousness, because, first, we do not really know the answer, and second, singers do not have to be persuaded that they are conscious. We can simply accept that most neuro-scientists now think that the mind is what the brain does.

For the singer, an important result of being conscious is the slow accretion of memories. We now know that memory is not stored in separate brain compartments. It is spread throughout the cortex, perhaps throughout the higher brain. This ability to store and retrieve memory is important in two ways. First, memories of relevant past experience, all of which are tinged with some emotion, can be called up to add nuances of expression to both the music and poem of a song. Second, the ability to memorize vast quantities of music and lyrics of songs and stage works is of the utmost necessity for a career singer. Think of Marilyn Horne having given 1300 recitals, or Placido Domingo learning 111 operatic roles! We learn both technique and music by adding and understanding one memory after another.

So this remarkable consciousness, with its memories of our past experience linked to the accompanying emotions, is where our "self" resides. This self knows who we are in the present, in the past, and on this concept of our self and our abilities we can make plans for our future. This self in action is our personality. We will take up more of this work for and by the self in later chapters.

Consciousness allows the singer to become aware of whether he is using his body efficiently. The chapter on mind/body will look at the problems of efficiency being lost in later life's tensions.

VOCAL SELF-PERCEPTION

One more ability of our musical brain is how we hear music, and how the singer hears his own singing. John Haskell's article on *Vocal Self-Perception* outlines two levels. Level I is self-monitoring of sensory feedback of vocal production, both auditory and tactile. Our musical brain adds up sensations of touch, pressure, movement, and position, from all parts of the vocal tract and any supporting structures.

Level II he labels "vocal self-identification". "On this level, vocal self-perception is the monitor of an acoustic and physiologic pattern that comprises a vocal set. This is learned behavior determined by such factors as vocal models (family, peers, etc.), cultural appropriateness, self-concept, attitudes toward one's own voice . . . The vocal set can be monitored and controlled on a conscious level but usually is not".

This Level II is a most important matter for a singer. Only the very rare lucky and highly talented singer will grow up with a vocal set that is also the most healthy and the most beautiful sound he could make. Rosa Ponselle may have been such a one, but most of us need to make that conscious effort to modify the set toward health and beauty. Psychologically this can be a great problem, because the first vocal set and our perception of it is so entwined with our self-concept of how we should sound, and with our identity. Singers' feelings of how they produce sound are notoriously imaginative, though they must be taken into account. To them, change seems undesirable, and education must proceed gently.

Both the teacher and the voice student must understand all they can of the relationship between self-perception and the physiology of voice production. The difficulty comes in being able to accept a new identity with a new voice.

On this matter of self-perception, Placido Domingo said: "I sing imperfectly, compared to what I have in mind. I know exactly how one should sing, every phrase, every note. I don't think

I will ever be able to do it. I wish I could". Of course, he sings very well, but he is sure it could be even better.

MEMORY AND MEMORIZING

A singer's brain must put together two kinds of memory, two functions. He must on the one hand call up the memory of the poetic text chiefly from the left hemisphere. On the other hand, the musical memories of the song come chiefly from the right hemisphere. Again, what a marvelous brain to be able to put these two sources together seamlessly. So marvelous we really think we are not doing so much after all.

We do know we are doing something special when we combine singing with movement on stage. Again, there are two chief memory maps in that musical brain: one has the memory for motor or procedural skills learned through practice. The other map has the memory for cognitive, or intellectual, abilities, such as remembering our music. It is the cerebellum, the "little brain", that controls motor coordination and posture. Intellectual or cognitive learning is linked to the hippocampus, which is part of the limbic system, the brain's center for emotions.

Gustav Mahler stated that he felt the need to express himself in music only when "indefinable emotions make themselves felt", and if they could have been expressed in language he would have done so. Thus, when there are two memories, one of music and one of words, we must realize we can have feeling for the meaning in the music (as did the composer), but we cannot truthfully put into words what it is. We can, I hope, shed some light on this early meaning when we consider the singer's early development.

We do need to know how to store these linguistic and musical forms, so that we can recall them. So how can we work to memorize songs in the shortest time and with the greatest strength of recall?

First of all, we need to have the healthiest sort of life style.

Not just so we can say "singers are athletes", though this is very true. We need this lifestyle so that our brain has the right amount of the neuro-transmitter serotonin. Serotonin aids and abets learning and memory formation. As serotonin is released in response to a stimulus, it attaches to the receptors of the next cell, raising its excitability level and increasing the chance it will become part of a circuit that encodes memory. Serotonin also enhances the neuron's electrical impulse, creating enduring memory.

Serotonin is the leader which choreographs the output of the brain. Therefore singers should eat breakfast, get enough sleep, get plenty of B vitamins, do releasing exercises, etc. etc. Their psychological state then will be kept more at the ready.

So now to the memorizing. Just being able to improve this will lessen a young singer's frustration. Let's first think about what has to be memorized: the melody, the rhythm, the accompaniment and especially the entrances, the tempo and thus the phrasing, the text, and altogether, the interpretation. Memorizing should not begin until one has settled all these preparations in the mind. Memorizing goes much faster when you know what you are doing. Rote learning invites a performance disaster.

When ready, some basic rules will help. To memorize a word that has no meaning for you is hard, so whether it is in your own or a foreign language, look it up. For some, it helps to write out the song text in longhand, then carry it with you all day. Others will need to have notes and words together. In the course of the day, look at this to see where you don't remember the melody or the rhythm or coordination with the accompaniment. Look it up in the score before the next day. Actually writing the text as well as just thinking or reading it gives strength to the memory for some. It is good, too, to silently repeat the words.

Some songs have descriptive phrases in which one thing and then another and another is mentioned, and to remember the order in which they come is difficult. For this, it is helpful to "make a film" running in your head, where you visualize each thing or place mentioned. When you've made this "film", it will only run in the same order as the song. Mnemonics may also be used, memorizing the first letter or word of each phrase.

Another rule is not to work too long at one time. Memory stores better in a fresh brain. Half an hour at a time works well. If one needs to work longer, a break of five minutes but not more than ten each half hour also works. The magic number 7 shows up in the ability of the short-term memory to store only 7 unrelated bits of information for about 20 seconds. Then it is either encoded in long-term memory or it decays and disappears. The amount of information that can be kept from decay can be increased by "chunking". That is, by grouping several bits of related information into a chunk, then seven chunks can be remembered. We can also forget information if for some reason we want to forget. In general, you will remember information longer if you absorb it gradually—spread out over as much time (days or weeks) as you have before performance.

If you are working on fast-note music, it is probably wise to take it somewhat slower at the very first. Remember to remember what vowel you are singing, and on fast coloratura material once you know the notes do not think of the notes but mentally repeat the vowel on each note of the run. This device plus very steady breath support gives the clearest production of runs.

If you like to learn a phrase at a time, always add to it the first few notes of the next phrase. This will allow you to remember "what comes next". If there is an instrumental interlude always add those first notes to your phrase memorizing.

Every song is a drama. We can take a page from our actor friends' book. Let your imagination call up images of both the external physical context and the inner world of emotions in the song. This imagery and the musical sound allied to it can strengthen the memory and its retrieval, and give a subtle performance.

Having in mind these basic rules, of which the most important is to do your memorizing in some place free from distraction, you are ready to prepare yourself for the actual work, by focused breathing and relaxation. Be patient, but concentrated on your task.

Hearing in silence is another good memorizing-practicing process. To hear in silence means to imagine vividly how your music sounds, so vividly that it is as if it were really being played and sung. The key to imagining is memory. It is amazing that when imagining music the brain lights up just the same as when actually hearing it.

The nine Greek muses were winged goddesses who presided over poetry, music, dancing and all the liberal arts. They were held to be the daughters of Jupiter and Mnemosyne. The word *mnemosyne* signifies *memory*. Therefore, poets have rightly called memory the Mother of the Muses. It is of course the *muse* who aids in the production of *music*, and looks after visual arts in *museums*.

PERFECT PITCH

Another ability of some musical brains is to recognize a pitch perfectly every time, and name it. It seems the average person has some internal sense of the absolute pitch of a note, since one study found that people consistently sing familiar songs in roughly the same key.

The musician's brain processes music differently. As mentioned earlier, studies indicate that non-musicians process music with the right half of the brain, the auditory, the pattern-recognizing half. Musicians too do so, but they also use the left half which handles language and therefore the ability to name. A recent study at the Heinrich Heine University in Düsseldorf, Germany, showed that in people with absolute pitch, part of the left hemisphere, the left temporal lobe, is especially well-developed relative to the symmetrical area in the right hemisphere. This area is next to or overlaps regions that handle auditory sound and language understanding. It may be that perfect pitch is a function of the language processing of the left side of the brain, because these musicians can name each tone they hear.

In addition, it is possible that having absolute pitch needs early exposure to music, since most who have it began musical study before age 6 or 7. None in a large study had it who started study after age 11. I have found this ability can be a psychological handicap for a learning singer. In the process of opening up a singer's range especially on the high side, the teacher can usually, when things go well, lure the student into vocalizing higher than he realizes and in a free way. Once done correctly, it can be done again. This ploy will not work when the student has absolute pitch. He immediately falls back on his old feeling that he cannot sing that high. Nevertheless I always have students stand where they cannot see what I am doing at the keyboard, so most of them cannot track what new tessitura they are establishing. The same goes for a soprano's low notes.

SPACE-TIME TRAINING

A study by Gordon Shaw, at the University of California Irvine, showed that music lessons coupled with a special computer program significantly increased the math skills of children at an inner city elementary school. Learning to play piano and learning how to read music helped the children to recognize rhythmic values, note values, and to identify letter names—E,G,B,D,F—from a note's scale placement. The computer program included spatial exercises such as assembling pieces of a puzzle and arranging geometric figures in particular orders.

The study showed that the learning of music emphasizes thinking in space and time, which leads to above average skills in spatial concepts found in mathematics, architecture, and engineering.

Dalcroze Eurythmics also still works in this area of musical awareness and training, in space-movement and time-rhythm. Perception is sharpened through "games", each of which has a musical meaning. Information on Dalcroze is listed in Supplement C.

THE POWER OF MUSIC

It is clear that the musical brain has capacities that help to explain the great power of music and the work of the singer to reveal that power. Part of that power and beauty are due to the large or small emotional tinges in the music and the words. The fine singer Helen Donath told me this story: "When I think of the last evening of songs in which my husband Klaus accompanied me as usual, and in which we performed many serious and sad songs, texts of Friedrich Ruckert: *I have finished with the world, At Midnight*, or the Brahms folk song *Down there in the Valley* where it says "the stars want to weep with me, one hears no bird's song nor joyful sound in the air, the wild animals are also sad with me among the stones and cliffs"—then I saw how an old lady in the audience pulled out a handkerchief. She was really crying. And it was only a simple folk song. It moved her so deeply that something in the heart of this woman must have been set free. She could weep and find some relief in it".

By the age of six months we already recognize the musicality of language, the combination of tonal sounds and pre-verbal meaning. Our hearing is one sense we cannot turn off, which partly accounts for music's power. Music physically moves us, and we notice an incongruity in sound immediately, with quite an incredible fineness of response. Just because we have such exquisite musical discrimination, for example, we recognize voices on the telephone of people we know but cannot see.

Every time we sing or play music we travel through a hierarchy of our own internal physiological and psychological evolution, our common humanity, and our personal experience. When we are the listeners this is what we are offered by the musician. People, when they learn I am a voice teacher, tell me "I can't carry a tune in a basket". But the truth is we are all musical, and everyone with a healthy voice can sing and improve their singing. Louis Botto, director of the group Chanticleer, says: "What people are looking for is a way to express or get in touch with their spiritual essence". This is what the singer and the sung-to are about, and it is this that our musical brain gives us. The brain runs the show.

—Music is a mathematically ordered structure of vibrations through time.

—(but) Like billowing clouds, like the incessant gurgle of the brook, the longing of the spirit can never be stilled.

—Hildegard von Bingen

CHAPTER II

It don't mean a thing
If you ain't got that swing

—Duke Ellington

MIND/BODY OF THE SINGER

All our thoughts, feelings, attitudes, beliefs, desires, dreams make up our inner world. We now are ready to look at the relation of our mind to our body, and how the give and take between them builds up our knowledge and concepts of our self and of our outer world.

Let us look at the body's workings as an interface between the inner and outer worlds that we sing about, in the order of their importance for a singer.

BREATHING

First without doubt is our breathing, a constant interaction with our environment, and needed to sustain life and to fuel the vocal instrument. It is true that to breathe well for singing is a technical matter, but it is also true that the mind set affects the breathing and it in turn affects the mind set. That is, if the singer feels the breath is right, the command for the onset of sound is easy. Or if the singer's mind is disturbed or unfocused, the body's attempt at making the sound is not its possible best. So we can work from both sides: to calm and clear the mind, and energize and ease the body. I had one student who had never heard the word "vocalise" before starting lessons, and who for some time thought I was talking about "vocal ease". What a delightful "error"!

Since we need to base our descriptions and imagery on fact, we should not speak of "diaphragmatic support", since the diaphragm relaxes while one is singing. Donald Proctor's summary of the singer's breathing: "In singing a sustained tone or phrase of low to moderate intensity after a deep breath in, we apply appropriate inspiratory effort to reduce subglottic pressure to the desired level. Next we steadily reduce that effort, and finally then apply a steadily increasing expiratory effort through the abdominal muscles. Slightly more expenditure of lung volume is required for very loud and very soft tones".

More Proctor on breathing: "My efforts will be to demonstrate to you that the beautiful voice which can carry to fill a large hall is the result, not of exertion of great power, but rather of delicate control of the power".

This is not the place to discuss details of the technical work of how to take and release the breath, but to note that any breath less than well managed immediately affects the psyche's attitude and attention, because the resulting sound is not easily given.

Paola Novikova, my great teacher, had us straddle a chair backwards, with arms and hands either resting on top of the chair back, or with elbows on knees and hands hanging down relaxed. She taught us, as I explain in detail in my book on *Building the Voice as an Instrument*, to "keep the ribs out" as long as possible while singing a phrase (Proctor's inspiratory effort) and then control the abdominal muscles as Proctor describes. Once this is automatic, students rather feel as though they are doing nothing to make the sound.

Paola told me a story, that her husband vocal coach Werner Singer had joked with her; "Why do these people line up at the door to work with you, when you only tell them to do nothing?!" This "nothing" really leaves the body free to make its complex coordinations. In short, our body is far more capable than we often give it credit for. What we have to learn is how to leave it free to do the work our mind wants, and this is not the same as "relaxation".

Robert Sataloff, in a presentation at the Voice Foundation's 1992 Symposium on the Care of the Professional Voice, said that the idea for a vocal sound originates in the cerebral cortex and travels to motor nuclei in the brain stem and spinal column, which coordinate the activities of the larynx, thoracic and abdominal muscles, and vocal tract articulators. The glottis closes, opens, changes shape, so its air resistance changes nearly continuously. These are rapid, complex adjustments to maintain a steady tone quality. The nerves provide auditory and tactile feedback to the brain.

All this happens due to our brain's compact message: consonant, vowel, intensity, tempo, timbre, meaning. Then the feedback allows us to make instant tiny adjustments in our conscious concepts and this message goes back to the vocal instrument, and so on continuously. The sub-glottal breath pressure is carefully planned.

Breathing is a rhythmic, continuous body experience which is consciously accessible. Since the body can take its time to breathe from one moment to the next, the action yields what Michael Eigen calls an unpressured sense of self, an experience of being. The ego finds support in breathing's constancy. On the other side, respiratory inhibition is a psychological mechanism for suppressing anxiety and repressing feeling. If a singer is too anxious, this must be reduced before the breathing can become full and rhythmic.

For any singer not yet clear about his/her breathing, there are breath references in the bibliography. Not all good singers understand their breathing. For instance, early on after Luciano Pavarotti was singing major roles in major houses, he was appearing with Joan Sutherland in Australia. He asked her to help him understand how she attained such fabulous steady control. Remember, the beginning of good control of breathing is in the mind, which sends correct messages until that breathing becomes automatic.

THE SENSES: HEARING, TOUCH

It is our senses that allow us to connect our outer and inner worlds. We so take for granted this environmental information and of our acting upon it, we forget how the senses are managing this collecting for the brain to interpret.

To make a comparison, zoologists tell us an elephant has a trunk with 40,000 nerves to feel out its neighborhood. This knowledge received in the elephant's mind provides the base for a complex system of vocal communication, in twenty-five different bellows, screams, barks, snorts, roars, growls and rumbles. Too, twenty-five distinct messages can be carried by the fifteen different purrings of a cat.

In the human body, there are five million neurons to carry information from our sense organs to the central nervous system, and some few hundred thousand to carry information away from the central nervous system to the various muscles of the body.

The most important senses for the singer are hearing and touch, with of course a good vision needed to read music and recording contracts, and to find one's way around a stage set. A singer must have auditory and kinesthetic feedback in order to regulate the pitch, the vowel, the feeling of resonance, and the emotional timbre.

Similarly, the voice teacher must have a hearing sensitive to everything a student's tones are telling him or her, and particularly to the overtones that create the vowels with maximum clarity and resonance. For the singer and the teacher to further sensitize their hearing calls for concentration. One method for developing a keener hearing has been devised by the French otolaryngologist Dr. Alfred Tomatis, whose work will be discussed in the last chapter.

We first heard or felt sound in utero. We felt our mother's steady heart beat, and the waves of her respiration. This fixes for a lifetime our most comfortable tempo and rhythm. This gives us the possibility of being soothed by waves of music. We will always feel an inexplicable twinge of anxiety when beats, rhythms, waves are somehow "not right". This is why we sing about a "sweet-heart".

We do hear music with our bodies. One example is having that chill run up and down one's back when musical meaning becomes so intense to the listener. I had a convincing experience of this in St. Paul's Cathedral in London. We had come in just at the end of a service, and went forward to sit in one corner of the apse to listen to the postlude. There, the organ's musical vibrations seemed to pour down the walls, and I heard (felt) them with my whole body in a most thrilling way. The mind that experiences and reacts to music is deeply embedded in the biology of the nervous system.

Diane Ackerman, in her delightful and informed book *A Natural History of the Senses,* tells about a creation myth sacred to the Maya, that the first human creatures to appear on earth were "Jaguar of the Night", "Mahucutah the Not Brushed", and "Jaguar of Sweet Laughter". They all had one thing in common: they could speak. If speech defines us as human, even more so does music-making and sweet laughter song. Sounds of all kinds captivate us, and we make sounds in harmonic frequencies out of our earliest experience. Noise, a sound that contains all frequencies, irritates us. Ackerman points out that it is fortunate we do not hear low frequencies very well. If we did, the sounds of our own bodies would be deafening.

Out of our pre-natal experience we also retain the soothing feeling of our body touched everywhere and buoyed by the amniotic fluid. This makes body massage, being touched, a premier way of shedding tensions.

The singer's major touch experience in the vocal tract is what we have for long indiscriminately called "placement". To appreciate what our kinesthetic sense can do for us, we need at least a simplified understanding of vocal acoustics. That is, to gain a resonant vowel on a given pitch, the singer establishes a certain jaw opening and a certain tongue and vocal tract position. When optimal, this space increases the energy in the one or two formants (overtones) which give a specific vowel its identity. The surest way to establish these "certainties" is not to try to set muscles for these positions, but to gain them through a clear mental concept of the vowel needed. During the learning of how to produce a resonant sound (and this is the only way a true legato is made), careful playing with tiny increments of jaw opening and of tongue position will establish the truly correct space for each vowel/pitch. When this happens the singer gets a wonderful feeling of vocal tract fullness, caused by the harmonically related air waves cycling through the tract. Gaining this resonant phrasing adds immeasurably to both the ease and expressiveness of singing. This makes, in short, a psychologically happy singer.

Our outer world is brought into our mind's consciousness by touch, hearing, vision, and our inner world adds language, memory, higher thought, attention and emotion. We do not know how all this extensive detail is coordinated, but we have seen that the cerebellum may be doing most of this work. We do know that practically all incoming sensory messages (except smell) go first to the thalamus, so that between the work of the cerebellum and the thalamus, plus the processed data from the cortex and emotion centers, we know what our mind/body is thinking and doing.

MOTION, SENSES OF BALANCE, SPACE, AND TIME

Once the outer world data and inner world requests have been collected and coordinated, this mind/body that is ourself identifies a need and moves to meet that need. We move also to keep our balance and not let gravity cause us to fall. Again, we are not aware of what a colossal feat this is. Think about the four environments in which we live. Discover magazine (Sept 2000, 50) gives some astonishing data on this.

First there is the earth rotating on its axis, the day and night circadian motion. Anything on the surface of the earth at say the New York City latitude is turning at the rate of 800 miles an hour. Then also as the earth makes its yearly orbit around the sun, it hurtles through its space in our galaxy at 66,600 miles per hour every hour. It is amazing to think that as we stand fairly still on a stage singing for an hour, both we and our audience have "flown" 800 miles in one orbit and 66,600 in another.

To realize the strength of gravity to keep us in our place, we can think of the moon orbiting the earth at the rate of 50,000 miles per day, so that the gravity play between earth and moon is such that the great oceans are pulled up to cause high tides to come in and go out from the shores. This pull plays on us as well, and if we add the movement through space of our entire galaxy, we are moving four ways at once. Yet every performer, singer, actor, dancer, athlete, must make that balance seem sure and must move from one position to another with grace.

It is surprising that the sense of hearing was originally a sense of gravity (Ackerman). The residue of this connection is found in the ear's work in maintaining our sense of balance. We are not aware of our hurtling through space, but these cosmic movements give us some sense of space and time, and it is within these forces and cycles that we stand and move and sing.

To insure a calm understanding mind we need a body that is strong and flexible. A singer needs a certain posture for a full breathing and the feeling that his whole body is expressing the sound—"singing from the toes". We speak of singers as athletes, but often something in our psychology keeps us from actually educating and strengthening our body and the neuronal pathways that control it. This neglect is brought on by being "too tired", "too busy", "too bored".

Once the singer breaks through these inhibitions, a number of interesting and oh so fruitful movement trainings can be investigated and some worked into his schedule. These include Benson's Progressive Relaxation, Alexander Technique, Feldenkrais, Tai Chi, Trager's Mentastics, and Yoga. The Dalcroze method, too, in its Eurythmics games, combines the joy of rhythmic movement with development of new musical perceptions.

Since many readers of this book are already familiar with these disciplines, I will put descriptions of and references to them in an appendix, for those not familiar with all of them.

There is a special relationship among movement and the senses of pleasure and of time, because these perceptions of pleasure and time share many brain circuits with the neurology of movement. This is why dancing is such fun.

I witnessed the profound effect such movements can have in releasing body/mind tensions and mental anxieties at a workshop of the National Association of Teachers of Singing. We had spent good time learning and doing Trager "Mentastics" exercises under the tutelage of a Boston University teacher. Then the group was asked who would like to sing, and a soprano volunteered to be first. She did sing, very well. Upon finishing the beautiful song, she sat right down on the stage floor in the bend of the piano and sobbed. It was the first time she had truly felt free to sing.

It is important for the teacher not to go directly to "fixing" the posture of a student. "Fixing" can substitute one tension for another and add to frustration. Training in Alexander Technique, for instance, will cause the body to properly balance itself, move on the balance, and stand well. Tai Chi, too, brings a lovely feeling of fluidity. Studio mirrors can give students helpful feedback about their body attitude.

Jan de Gaetani, a fine singer and teacher, would start her class for singers by having them lie on the floor and begin moving various parts of their bodies while holding the rest of themselves immobile. Slowly, they discovered their own particular tendencies to lean right or left, to tense muscles that are not needed, or to overextend parts of their chest or back.

This is far from being just body work. It is body/mind work—the brain in command of what the body does, the body's feelings and actions guiding the psyche to success or failure or something in between. De Gaetani said "What you do with your body affects your entire musical view. The purpose of these exercises is to make the body as efficient a vehicle for the voice as possible".

Another route for training body expressiveness is to take a modern dance class. I was lucky to get a year of Saturday classes with Hanya Holm and her then first assistant Alwin Nikolais. I didn't become a dancer, but I learned how to get on stage without falling apart. It is certain that being in more control of movement helps one's confidence.

Such body/mind training can contribute to the performer's control over the subtle duration of the sounds he makes and of the rests or silences in his song, generally called *timing*. Timing is usually related to rhythm, which is important for both melody and harmonic progression. Studies show that the time course of different partials in a tone is critical for the perceived timbre. Alf Gabrielsson in Sloboda's book on *Generative Processes in Music* in referring to traditional musical terminology, suggests categories of the structural, the motional, and the emotional aspects of musical experience. The artist's timing will affect the motion character of the music and its related emotional qualities. We have already seen that the individual singer will settle on his own comfortable tempo for a song in a given style, on which he will practice an expressive timing.

Ingo Titze has some fascinating thoughts about the natural

frequencies in our bodies, that "the body must carry out its natural oscillatory functions around vocal fold vibration. We can either fight these other oscillations or use them to our advantage". It is the mind/body that does the oscillating, the fighting or the using. It don't mean a thing, if you ain't got that rhythm. But in physical and psychological health we all have got that rhythm.

EMOTIONS

With senses working, mind coordinating, and body moving, we get what we call e-motion. We say "I am touched" about something. "I am moved" equates motion and emotion. "I feel jumpy". "I hear you" meaning "I empathize". To say that now we get to the heart of the matter is already a revealing metaphor.

Our songs are about feelings and thoughts. The melody and harmony of a song cannot be verbalized, turned into words. But the lyric says sometimes I feel like a motherless child. Sometimes I know where I'm goin' and I know who's goin' with me. Alleluia! and joy to the world!

Chansons triste, then happy days are here again and I got rhythm and make a joyful noise. Ich Liebe Dich, but love is a wild bird. Still, calm as the night and deep as the sea shall your love be. Well, my love is green as the lilac bush and my soul has wings of the nightingale. Later, the time of lilacs and the time of roses is past.

The music, inspired in the composer by a poem, has emotional meanings based on and embedded in the experiences of infancy and early childhood. These are non-verbal expressions of great wants, needs, and satisfactions, which we will look at further in the context of childhood musical development. Before we cognitively analyze a piece of music as we hear it and gain an emotional realization of its structure, we may have an unnameable emotion. T.S. Eliot, in *The Dry Salvages* puts it:

> music heard so deeply
> That it is not heard at all, but you are the music
> While the music lasts.

The singer who sings of emotions must have a strong memory and a strong sense of self. To attain this sense of self is a difficult, a most complex, a most rewarding work. He must have a mind that will settle on or has settled on an identity: "I am one who sings". This involves a clear feeling of the self as mind/body that can function as a whole to produce a sound this self can accept.

Why we need to bother knowing about how the brain works, what our mind does with this work, and relation of brain/mind to mind/body, is this very basic need of a singer's acceptance and elegant use of this body/mind/self to produce song.

Antonio Damasio helps us understand the impact of emotion on cognition, and he believes that emotion can be an aid to reasoning. So an atmosphere of positive emotion combined with a system of appropriate reward is conducive to learning. He says the brain organizes thoughts by assigning values to them. "Value is just another way to talk about emotion".

Somehow, in ways not yet totally understood, information about the physical state of our body and the psychological state of our mind and the movements we make in action and reaction to our environment all come together to give us the awareness of self, a self-consciousness. The embodied self will remain as the core that situated the self in the world and acts as a personal frame of reference for cognitive, linguistic, and culturally defined aspects of self. We know ourselves as spatial, persisting objects. We also know ourselves as subjects that feel and think. There is an elusiveness in this idea, that in addition to a flesh and blood person, we must recognize a metaphysical or transcendent subject, which seems essentially not an object at all.

The persona this self-knowledge gives us, something spatial, something emotional, something cognitive, has this persisting core, with various elements coming to the surface to be the masks with which we face our changing world. This egocentric frame of reference gives us literally and metaphorically a point of view from which to operate. Here lies the basis of our work as actor/ singer. We have an embodied mind and a minded body, with feeling.

The singer has several interests in understanding emotion. The better he understands his own current emotions, the better he can manage and make use of them. The more sensitive the singer is to some deep feeling underlying his own and his song's emotions the better he can describe them and tune the timbre of his song. His third concern about emotion is what or how much he can convey through song to his audience. His simulated but felt expression of the emotion he finds in song music and text is what we call interpretation. Finally, he needs a ready emotional intelligence in order to meet the demands of a singer's life: to get on well with a manager, with colleagues, coaches, conductors, stage directors, friends and relations.

Anthony Storr, psychiatrist and amateur pianist-violist, believes music probably developed from the crooning, cooing tones and rhythms in the vocal but nonverbal exchanges between mothers and infants, and that this helps explain its power to make us weep or exult. I would add that the infant's early cooing and crying is an intense emotional expression, the meaning of which is stored in the infant's receptive growing brain. We will look further at this deep nonverbal memory when we study the early development of sound-making. Music becomes an abstract representation of and stimulus to such a surge of emotions as occurred in childhood.

Storr points out that musical emotion differs from the genuine feeling in its reassuring orderliness. He writes: "We crave it partly for its power to structure our auditory experience and thus to make sense out of it". Finding and creating pattern is a deep-rooted human instinct. Song melodies have both a horizontal (timing) and a vertical (formants) structure. Storr's thesis is that we crave music both for the unruly passions it lets loose, and for the rule it imposes on them.

Much of modern life has us separating rational thought from feelings. Music reunites the mind and body, and through either hearing or performing it we can regain some sense of wholeness.

Over millennia we have developed what Yale University psychologist Peter Salovey in 1990 was the first to call an "emotional IQ". He and Daniel Goleman define this as the ability to know oneself, to recognize feelings of rage and anxiety, sadness and joy, and to empathize these feelings in others. Goleman thinks emotional intelligence encompasses traits such as self-awareness, empathy, optimism, impulse control, and the ability to handle anger and anxiety. These traits stem from both nature (inborn qualities of temperament) and nurture (by home and family and school). Fortunately these traits can be developed further at any time in life, as reported by Craig Lambert (Harvard Magazine, September 1998, 10).

The teacher of singing has a good chance to help students improve their emotional intelligence, if the teacher's E.I. is at a level where his/her empathy, enthusiasm, fairness and gentle control reaches the student's awareness and helps him respond in kind to teacher and peers.

We can hear in the performing situation the study the singer has made of the composer's and poet's emotions. How much of the performer's emotional message can be conveyed to and experienced by the audience? The British Journal of the Society for Research in the Psychology of Music and Music Education (19, #2) has four articles reporting experiments on emotional response to music. These and other studies show that "happiness" or "sadness" are well recognized, whereas "fear" and "anger" are more difficult to name. "Shivers run down the spine" with an accompanying emotion of pleasure are most often evoked by passages containing new or unexpected harmonies. Tears were more reliably evoked by the repetition more than twice of a melodic motif and by appogiaturas.

In portraying emotion, singers need to realize that a brilliant or vocally perfect high note is the result of innate or acquired skill, which makes its own effect. A singer can show emotion best in any lower notes, and particularly in register transition notes. Singers must carefully plan their portrayal of a character's emotions, but also must not allow the "real" emotion to take charge and upset their performance. We will study this in context in the chapter on performance.

Emotion derives from e-movere, to move away from, that is, to move from neutral. I. Fonagy reports in *Research Aspects in Singing* on twenty years of study of prosodic expression in emotional speech:

> Anger is expressed by forceful expiration, imperfect
>   phonation, heavy stresses, dark vowel color.
> Longing, by a gradual increase and decrease of intensity,
>   by pitch frequency rises and falls, ending with
>   slight final rise.
> Fear, by narrow pitch range, a contracted body, low
>   vocal intensity, and breathy voice.
> Female Coquette, portrayed by sudden switches to head
>   register to mock, tease, or flirt; using a half
>   whisper to show concealed passion.

R.S. Coleman reports a study of how well a random group of listeners could identify the emotions portrayed by four professional actors. The actors read the same nonsense material to variously show "joy", "terror", "grief", and "contempt", by dynamics, manner, and tone quality. The average score for correct identification was 84%. It was 91% for grief and contempt, and in the high 70's for joy and terror. Singers, too, can learn to vary their manner, dynamics and tone quality in portrayal of emotion.

BODY MESSAGES

When e-motion erupts into motion, we see what is generally called "body language". I prefer to call it body messages since these are nonverbal and not produced by tongue movement. We can now consider how a performer's nonverbal signals add to or distract from the message of a song's music and poetry. The dynamic levels and tempo of emotional feeling in the music ask the singer for further expression by body and face, adding important meaning to the song.

The singer expresses the meaning that the music and text and emotional tone have for him. The audience takes in all of this they can and decides on the meaning that it has for them. So the gift is not of one emotion from the singer to the hearer, but a gift of the singer's devotion to the meaning for himself. This can fire a new nonverbal self-understanding in the hearer.

Operating parallel to this need to express is a need to protect ourselves. Many of us do not wish to bare to the world our deepest strongest feelings both known and unknown to us. This results in some masking of our true feelings, so that generally we express only the surface feelings of which we are aware, and only what we believe those in our environment will accept without too much fuss. A favorite mask is a smile.

Our unconscious body messages and the way we mask what we need to, plus our general demonstration of the way we think we are, results in our *persona*. This persona is our personality as seen and heard by others, and our *self-image* as seen by ourself.

In the ancient Greek theater the actors wore masks and said their lines through the mask. This speaking through the mask establishes then the "per-sona", the "through-sound". So we have the following relations:

> unconscious body messages
> to persona (self-image, personality)
> to persona (through-sound)

to persona (career masks, real life masks)
to persona (stage acting).

The study of body messages (body language, body talk) is called kinesics, which has the Greek root meaning movement. Kinesics is defined as motion as related to speech, so that our body messages either reflect and enhance what our speech is saying, or may tell the viewer that what we mean is just the opposite of what we say. If we send an ambiguous total message, the viewer may easily misunderstand our meaning.

It is a long term problem for the singer to gain control of his body messages. First, for good training, he must send true messages to his teacher, as well as learn to read his teacher's messages accurately. I found in teaching that if the student did not work on the meaning of his song right from the start, that singer would think so strongly about his technique that in performance his face would end up expressionless, "deadpan".

Conveying a full meaning of the song is what we call interpretation. I have always been a little careful with this word, and would help students to concentrate on both the surface and the deep meaning of the words and the music, and not "pour chocolate sauce over them". Body armor can be removed, new understanding reached, so that we can unmask some true feelings. If one grasps the meanings, one's emotional nature will respond and these meanings can be expressed.

A big difference between singing a recital or a stage work is that for the stage there is a director, who shows the singer/actor the movements and expressions he wants. Of course the singer adds his share of ideas, but the recitalist must plan, for every one of his some twenty songs, the nonverbal expressions true to the character singing the song. He also must allow expression of the joy he has in sharing with his audience. Opera has far less of this attention to audience because the singers usually must not break their reactions to the ensemble on stage. Here the audience is tied in to the drama of the ensemble and the orchestra, as well as the passion of each singer. NATS member Matt Bean's articles as listed in the bibliography have much to say on these points.

My purpose here is not to detail what these unconscious body movements' messages are, nor what they mean, but chiefly to point out their importance so that more knowledge and control of them can be built into the early work with the singer—by a teacher, a coach, a drama director, and by the singer himself. Studies show that in a given message half may be made verbally, but at least 50% is nonverbal. Of this 50%, half of that is in facial expression. It is important to keep in mind that the meaning of a movement does not lie in itself but in its context of words, music, and situation.

It can be confusing to a singer to have various teachers and coaches offer different interpretations of the same motion. Let us note here only the various modes of nonverbal behaviour. They are: gestures, facial expressions, posture, sweating, blushing and blanching, style and manner of speaking/singing, tone of voice. These nonverbal expressions of attitude are partly instinctive, partly taught, and partly imitative.

Four references listed in the bibliography are an excellent help toward a better understanding of this complex signalling by the psyche. Here is a brief description of their offerings.

The first of these is a book by Robert Lange on *Unconscious Communication in Everyday Life*. Of the four writers he goes deepest into the origin of these forms of expression. Human communication is essential to survival, and Lange tells how we encode messages to protect ourselves. He discusses single and multiple message, surface message, encoding and decoding conscious and unconscious message, and finally meaning and non-meaning in messages that lie or tell the truth.

The second reference is an article by Susan Levasseur that takes up a whole issue of the Journal of Research in Singing, derived from her dissertation: *Nonverbal Communication in the Applied Voice Studio*. She notes that forces of power, control, influence, motivation, self-esteem and interpersonal meaning are all related to nonverbal expression. It seems there are many thousands of facial expressions, so the teacher may reveal in various ways what her expectations are for each student. Levasseur details many hand gestures teachers use to remind students of instructions made earlier, "because they watch the nonverbal communication by students to determine the extent of trust and the impact of their instruction directives".

One example of nonverbal gestures I used was to close the red open mouth of a small carved wooden dragon head, and let it drop wide open again—this of course only when the student forgot to give a "wide" vowel its due, and not used too often. Later a colleague sent me from Japan a flashy hand puppet dragon, which added amusement and point in a lesson. So my students called my studio the "Dragon Studio", not meaning me, of course.

Levasseur's description of all this interplay is most helpful. So is her picturing of how a singer or a teacher may control variables of nonverbal communication during an interview in order to gain a part, or a position.

In *Concert Song as Seen, Kinesthetic Aspects of Musical Interpretation,* Sara K. Schneider quotes the mime Marcel Marceau: "A gesture must be clothed in thought, not just a 'beautiful movement'". She notes that the beginning singer shows more of the *work* of singing than of the *meaning.* Solo singers have an extreme self-consciousness, and nervous singers may show a stiffly armored performing position. She quotes Pierre Bernac to remind us of the musical score's inadequacy to convey the living quality of the music. And anthropologist John Blacking: "The mind cannot be separated from the body . . . for it is in the areas of nonverbal communication, especially dancing and music, that we may observe a mind at work through movements of bodies in space and time". Schneider draws on the work of Antonia Lavane, of Shirlee Emmons, of Wesley Balk, and on her own performance theories, to make a very helpful analysis.

Finally, we turn to Wesley Balk's beautiful work to free singer/actors. In his first book *Performing Power* he was still working out ways of exercising the expressive modes: the Hearing/Vocal

Mode, the Facial/Emotional Mode, and the Kinesthetic Mode. His description of these in this book might be read first. His second book, second edition, *The Complete Singer/Actor*, gives a further development of exercising the modes. All three of Balk's books should be in every music library. His suggestions are far too extensive to report briefly,but any singer studying them will benefit greatly in stage presence and nonverbal expression, and therefore in interpretation.

A young singer working to improve his message or interpretation can do worse than study the fluidity of bodily expression shown in old silent films of Charlie Chaplin. I am sure his understanding of his movements' meanings will never be equaled, unless once more a silent film is made by a super actor. Other film actors who can teach us are Danny Kaye and Lily Tomlin.

Lotte Lehmann shall have the last word here on this subject, "Young singers . . . . should develop their own interpretations which should spring . . . . from their own minds. Imitation is the enemy of artistry . . . . Technique is the all-important foundation, the a b c of singing . . . . But realize technique must be mastered to the point of being *unconscious*, before you can really become an interpreter".

STRESS

We have seen how our breathing, our hearing and inner kinesthetic sense, our way of moving and body alignment, our emotions and nonverbal messages all are used in our expressive singing. If pulling all this together seems too demanding, remind yourself of your musical brain. Remember, it has a hundred billion neurons. Every neuron has some 10,000 possible connections to other neurons, which means there are possibly one million billion connections. If the neurons of the brain were put end to end they would be two million miles long. They carry messages continuously, several million messages a second, according to Richard Restak.

The better we understand how we function in these interactions of our mind/body/environment the more control we have of our performing behavior. We need to know how stress gets involved in vocal production. The singer experiences performance stress, but is also subject to life's general stresses. Beyond these, if he becomes a professional singer, are career stresses. Here we will consider the nature of the stresses of common life, and take up in later chapters the specific stresses of performance and career, where these can be understood in context.

When we say the word "stress" we are apt to think at once this is bad. Not all stress is bad. We can think of stress as a challenge we meet and manage, as a positive force for personal achievement and happiness. How can we, in Hans Selyes' words, have "stress without distress"?

Each demand on our body is unique and specific—e.g. when exposed to cold we shiver to produce more heat. But when one of the marvelous balances of our mind/body is thrown into imbalance, that mind/body must undertake a non-specific action to restore the balance. The mind/body must respond to a problem regardless of what that problem may be. This demand for adaptive activity is what we feel as stress, whether the situation we face is pleasant or unpleasant. The one thing that most affects the outcome in body-behavior and mind-memory is the intensity of the stress-producing activity, the stressor.

Unmanaged stress brings fatigue, anxiety, illness and burnout. Managed stress, that is, adapting successfully to the stressor, brings a sense of control of self and life, of balance, even of creativity. We know that a not-too-great rush of adrenaline enhances a singer's performance. There is a spectrum of physiological arousal ranging from Benson"s "relaxation response" at one end to the full "fight or flight" response at the other.

During maturation, as we meet the challenges of life's stresses, our voice is formed. This voice is the mirror of our personality, it is our self speaking, and it reflects emotions stirred in us by both good and bad stress. Not only can disturbances of physical function have profound emotional effects, emotions disturbed by stress can have bodily and artistic effects. Indeed, stress is a special problem for singers, whose delicate vocal instrument may be so affected it produces poor sound.

When stress is first felt, there are three questions to ask and three life-style needs to check. The questions are: (1) Does this threat really exist? (2) If so, is it worth a fight? (3) If so, can I make a difference? Then the life-style check: Am I getting (1) enough sleep? (2) proper nutrition? (3) hydration? Then one can generally sort through what can be and what cannot be controlled. It also helps to remind oneself of one's strengths and accomplishments.

Then one can take a walk to mull over the problem. Exercise activates the sympathetic nervous system, the system that raises the heart rate, increases oxygen intake, pumps adrenaline and releases glucose into the blood stream. It also stimulates the area of the brain that synthesizes endorphins, chemicals that put the "high" into a runner's high.

Slower movements such as Yoga or Tai Chi stimulate the parasympathetic nervous system, which lowers the heart rate and blood pressure and brings calm. Slow, calming, flowing movements can open up hidden emotions, and can teach us how to gain that total concentration a performer needs, which we describe as "being in the zone".

In addition to these movement programs, there are other ways to cope with stress such as massage, meditation, relaxation. To decide which would do the most to relieve our stress, we must decide "what is my stress style?" We must know whether our "style" is more mental, more physical, or a combination of both. If stress registers mainly in one's body, pick an exercise or a movement program. If mainly we feel invaded by worrisome thoughts, anything that redirects the mind should work. Meditation furnishes a very direct intervention, but so do everyday things such as reading, crossword puzzles, chess, or even vigorous exercise that unhooks the mind.

If, however, the stress lodges in both body and mind, choose any combination of movement and mind redirecting. However you feel, know that mind and body are inextricably linked in these adaptations to stress. A singer needs to know how to cope with stress almost as much as he needs correct technique, because the stress may ruin the technique.

A do-it-yourself massage is also effective, and in a short time much tension can be released, particularly in the face, neck and shoulders. Start with the temples, massaging gently in a circular motion, alongside each eye socket. Move to the forehead with light strokes. Stroke each side of the nose, then the cheeks from both sides of the nose toward the ears, then the face, then lightly behind the ears.

Find the areas of tension on either side of the neck at the base of the head. With a circular movement go into the scalp, and then down to where the neck and back meet. Take hold of the muscles on either side of the neck and squeeze. Move on to the top of the trapezius muscle, with the right hand working the left side and the left working the right.

Parts of this self-massage can be done in the middle of practice and rehearsals and even in lessons.

As researchers continue to study the communication between mind and body, they find the dividing line disappearing between what is biological and what is psychological.

The Stress Reduction Clinic at the University of Massachusetts Memorial Health Care Center conducts research on how the mind affects healing, and they make use of a Buddhist-type meditation called mindfulness as a supplement to Western medicine. Unlike the types of meditation which concentrate on a word, phrase, or image, mindfulness practice begins with paying attention to breathing. Finally, the meditator is taught to encounter his own "wholeness", and deal with illness, or what are felt to be threats, from the perspective of being complete.

Dr. Jon Kabat-Zinn says "Learning how to pay attention deepens our ability to concentrate and relax . . . . most of us waste enormous amounts of energy reacting automatically and uncon-sciously to everything we experience. Mindfulness gives you a range of ways to pay attention, so that when necessary you can go into deep states of inner calmness and stillness but still be functioning in the world. The path to mindfulness lies no further away than your own body, mind, and breathing".

Of great importance to the singer is the psychology involved in quieting the mind, in awareness that is not judgmental, in relaxed concentration, in "effortless" effort, in seeing what is and in awareness of what can be, in trusting one's self, in "letting it happen".

BODY IMAGE

In forty years of teaching I noticed a constantly recurring event. To sing vowels on a given pitch clearly and resonantly, it is necessary to drop the jaw, open the mouth, wide open for some vowels, half way for some, and very little for others. It was clear that some singers did not know how much they were opening. I would ask them to look in a small mirror, standing conveniently on the piano, for them to see what they were doing while they sang the vowel vocalize. They understood the acoustic reason why I asked them to do this. Yet, any number of them were very reluctant to look in the mirror. Though quite willing to make the mouth adjustment because they understood it brought more reso-nance, they still hated to look at themselves in the mirror in the presence of anyone else.

At first I didn't understand their problem, for to me they were all good-looking-enough kids. But here we are, at one of the most important mind/body concepts for the singer/actor. Gaining an acceptable body image is doubly important to performers, because it works two ways. The body image seen by the audi-ence will enhance or detract from the aesthetic effect of the performance. And, if the singer has a negative body image, that will undermine his performance.

Let us begin this story at the beginning. The development of a body image, a body self, begins at birth. The infant's body, its affects and movements, are first experienced both directly and through the mother's mirroring. All this falls together and the infant has no sense of a separate self. Gradually, a body-surface boundary is felt, and from a few months on into the walking stage a body self emerges from the realized body boundaries and perception of varied body states. It is critical that the infant's brain be able to make these perceptions and be able gradually to separate self from the environment. Much of the nature of this self will depend on how the infant is handled. Both D.W. Winnecott and Paul Piaget have helpful descriptions of this process.

By about 18 months the child has developed a full imaging capacity, so that what were transitional objects (not totally separated from self) can now be imagined when they are absent. Thus comes an early awareness of a body image with an integration of inner and outer experience.

This image of body experience is a combination of the external nature of one's physical appearance as seen by society, and the internal, subjective, representations of physical appearance and bodily experience. Thomas Cash and Thomas Pruzinsky point out that body image is really *body images* with the objective and subjective images combined. Freud said "The ego is first and foremost a body ego". Our body image has a close relation to our personality. So when people worry about how they look, they are worrying about who they are.

By around this 18-months-old time, the child achieves a definition and cohesion of body self as a foundation for self-awareness. This body self is *form*, with distinct patterns of behavior and systematic experience of reality. It is also a *concept*, an enduring inner frame of reference, comprised of bodily and emotional images, concepts, experiences. Over time this synthesis of body and psychological selves provides a unity and continuity through time, space, and various conditions.

To summarize, this sequence begins with the imaging and symbolizing of objects, then differentiation between self and object, leading to self-awareness. Taking time for this differentiation allows a space for contemplation and judgment between an urge and an action. Without this space, an action is reflexive, or impulsive.

Our physical appearance has much to do with how we are thought of by others. It can give information about gender, race, possible age, social status, economic level, and even occupation. All this we sort into categories and make some assumptions that lead to appearance stereotypes: that good-looking people are good, not so good-looking people are less good. Studies show that attractive people are thought to be happier, smarter, more successful, more interesting, more sociable, but also more self-centered and sex-typed. Sometimes women are unfairly thought to win success more because of attractive appearance than by skill or clear thinking.

At any rate, all of this is a general problem, since one-fourth of men and one-third of women have negative feelings about their appearance, according to studies by Thomas Cash. Those with negative body feelings reported lower levels of life satisfaction and self-concept.

Not only will such negative feelings handicap singers, those who think of themselves as overweight will suffer self-consciousness on stage. Often this body image of being overweight is incorrect and they suffer without reason. Fortunately, body images can be changed. In fact,they do change, and we adjust our view. A little conversation with a knowledgeable and empathetic friend or teacher may relieve the cognitive error. The goal is to bring self-perception of physical appearance in line with objective perceptions.

This feeling of unsure self can lead to trouble for singers. If they seek help, a therapist may use techniques and studies focusing on body-self development, such as viewing videotapes, or making dance movements, or other movement programs as described in Supplement C. Cash and Pruzinsky give further ways of dealing with this developmental arrest involving body self and body image.

Things you can do for yourself to improve body image:

(1) Try to be realistic about your appearance, learn to like yourself as you are.

(2) Treat yourself by following good nutrition and exercise plans.

(3) Ask yourself if making #(2) changes is important and how it will change your inner life, then set realistic goals for any changes you would like to make.

(4) Encourage family and friends to appreciate your efforts and to support you.

(5) Join in group activities with a common interest such as art, music, or sport.

Body image underlies self-esteem, and poor self-esteem or lack of confidence underlies performance anxiety. We will study this further in the context of the performance situation.

Our mind/body/self lives in an environment of both marvels and disappointments, and within us is the story of our life. All of this we sing about. We sing to tell what we cannot speak.

—The voice is the only instrument that is totally dependent upon a physical and psychological unity of instrument and performer.
—Richard Miller

—You do not sing yourself, your body sings you.
—Francesco Lamperti

—When I make music, I am praying.
—Duke Ellington

CHAPTER III

O wüsst ich doch den Weg zurück (Brahms)

MUSICAL DEVELOPMENT IN CHILDHOOD

EARLY EXPERIENCE

Now that we are more familiar with the brain and mind/body of a singer, we cannot leap forward to an understanding of the adult singer/performer/teacher without first going back to the beginning.

Childhood musical experience, as well as abilities and characteristics inherited in the genes, will make considerable difference in whether a child does or does not grow into being a singer. If he becomes a singer, these early musical exposures and practices will further, or if not present hold back, his technical and artistic abilities.

We have already noted that in utero we feel rhythms and hear sounds. Paul Michel and others have much to tell us about the optimal development of musical abilities in the first year of life which show what different bases each singer may have established, but also what changes in present music curricula in pre-school and early school might be productive.

Jean Piaget theorized that stages of development were dependent primarily on biological steps triggering effects at each age level. This can explain a great deal of development, but Michel has found that musical development is not rigidly fixed to age levels, and that the musical achievements of childhood have been considerably underestimated, and often not built on by family and school. Given these achievable musical abilities, it has long been my belief that anyone, everyone, could sing quite well (1) if they wanted to, and (2) thought they could.

What must be true of the budding musician is having an extra sensitivity to sound, its acoustic and sequential nature, such that the child senses the vibration, rhythm, tempo, duration, pitch, tone, and resonance. The child copes with this sensitive awareness, thus gaining more understanding of music, a defense for mastering the sensitivity. This talented child becomes passionate about his music, often cannot find words to express the passion, and must express it through some music-making. Parents and teachers have great responsibilities for these children or adolescents.

The first year of the infant is full of musical development. Michel shows that the first six months is the period of *learning to hear*. Overt reactions to sound arise very early. As the hearing analyzer and hearing brain centers develop, there is a noticeable increase in reaction to and a "pleasure in hearing" musical stimuli. The frequency of reaction doubles in the first four weeks! and increases steadily through the following months. In the second week, the child is quiet, unmoving for a short time in hearing a continuous acoustic stimulus. At two months he lies still in fixed attention if anyone sings, or plays an instrument. By five months this acoustic dominance can last as long as half an hour.

Not only does this acoustic attention develop, but Michel's tests show that the infant begins to distinguish between sounds according to pitch and timbre. The melodic contour (pitch pattern up and down) is the most important feature in melody perception from early infancy on.

In the second half of the first year of life the child can "hear" more and more accurately the sounds in its world. This growing "pleasure in hearing" later sends part of the general public to recitals, operas, musicals, concerts, and gets us to buy huge numbers of singers' CDs, tapes, musical videos and historical recordings.

Now we can relate the baby's early vocalizing to somewhat more sure causes. Pained crying must come from hunger, or a gastric feeling that won't burp, or wetness, or something pressing heavily on the body. If these problems are taken care of, there may be some sounds of satisfaction. Besides the crying, there is early cooing, which either is a response to or imitates mother/caretaker sounds, or is made for the sheer pleasure of sound-making and then hearing. This is the beginning of singing, as well as of expressive speech.

I want to stress here that all of these early sounds, which are nonverbal and whose meaning cannot be described easily in words, are tinged with emotions: pain, fear, anger, pleasure, attachment, the need to communicate. If this is true of the vocal sound and if non-percussive instruments were invented to imitate many vocal sounds, we can understand the great power of music to move us when we know not surely why.

The infant's, and adult's, memory of mother's heartbeat is not lost: slower than 72 beats per minute is relaxing, more than 72 is stimulating. Lullabies simulate slow breathing. The emotional impact of music heard or produced depends on the melody, the harmony, the timbre, the form. This structure of music generates tensions, so that we enjoy the release of this arousal when the music resolves into satisfactory harmony at its conclusion.

As the infant's cerebral cortex develops and people speak and sing to him, he begins to join in the mother's singing. Paul Michel reports children of 4 to 6 months singing some single notes correctly. He believes the baby discovers the effect of different pitches at this age and tries them out, so gradually making melodies out of unconsciously motivated baby sounds.

Kenneth Wright, basing his work on D.W.Winnecott's ideas, explores the visual experience of the gaze between mother and baby. He believes that the zone of the mutual gaze becomes the space of working and reworking, of the establishment of symbols, language, metaphor, and structure. This grasp of symbolic structure is an essential element in the growth of a musician.

At the age of about one year, though the age can vary widely, children begin to sing spontaneous songs. They keep a rhythmic regularity and elongate vowels, but do not yet have a sense of the pitch scale. At two years the typical song has a repetition at different pitch levels of a brief melodic phrase. For example, our son at age two improvised this song:

> If I were something
> I would say yes,
> Because it's fun.

Unfortunately, I kept no notation record. He had a recording telling about orchestral instruments, and one day I heard him say about music on the radio, "that's a cello". This had to be based on timbre recognition. A funnier remark when he heard a coloratura soprano: "That lady is making ha-ha squeaks".

If the child is provided with appropriate musical activities following strong development in the first year, he will develop hearing and listening ability in major and minor intervals or scales by the age of six, not so late as age twelve as was formerly thought.

John Sloboda says that high musical talent needs time to "mess around with itself". I would add that it is good psychology for an adult artist to allow himself some of the same sort of time.

Maria Manturzewska describes the first six years as Stage I in the development of professional musicians. Stage I, she says, is not homogeneous and has three sub-stages:

(1) within the first 15 months, formation and development of sensory-emotional sensitivity to sounds and music;
(2) 1½ to 3 years, development of cognitive sensitivity to acoustic and musical stimuli, and the development of categorical perception of pitch;

(3) 3 to 5 years, development of musical memory and imagination, and spontaneous vocal and instrumental activity.

In the first stage, it is important that there be one person in the environment who is emotionally related to the child and strongly interested in music, so that the child hears a great deal of quality music. Thus the child develops an emotional aesthetic and sensory-emotional sensitivity to music. An example is Renée Fleming—both her parents were singers.

In the second sub-stage the child identifies sounds in its environment and recognizes acoustic stimuli. It plays with and manipulates sounds, and recognizes tonal characteristics in instruments. This is the crucial time of categorical perception of pitch and the development of absolute pitch.

The 3 to 5 year sub-stage brings the development of musical memory and imagination. Future exceptional performers can sing many melodies, tap out their rhythms, compose songs, and play at being musicians, tapping out tunes on the piano or beating rhythms on pots. Hearing music, preferably live, is important. They may have an intense musical experience which they remember for life.

Manturzewska found an interesting correlation between first recollections and ultimate career: future performers gave more cognitive details about the music, and future music teachers had more aesthetic or emotional recollections.

She found that the entire Stage I was critical for the development of a natural musicality, an intuitive comprehension of musical language with a sensory-emotional understanding. This comprehension allows an easy fluency in both singing and playing. This is the optimum age for this kind of learning.

If this feeling of emotional ties to music and its spontaneous expression is not developed before the age of nine, exceptional abilities are not as likely to develop. Manturzewska says that one having first contact with music after the age of nine may become a professional musician, even a good one, but will probably never attain full ease in performance. This age-of-learning factor can be one of the deep causes of stagefright.

Stage II, between 6 and 8 years, is the time the child usually can begin systematic work with an instrument, and great progress is made between 10 and 14 years. Grace Mota's studies show that individual tests reveal musical attitude better than a standard aptitude test, and that randomly selected children do as well, with musical training, as those thought at first to be more talented. John Sloboda believes that difference in ability depends primarily on differences in musical experience, not on in-born talent.

The next Stage III Manturzewska labels the stage of formation and development of the artistic personality, during the years of ages 14 to 18 or 20. We will explore this further in the chapters on adolescent singers and performance.

There are many vicissitudes in a talented child's development. He may feel like a loner, because he is "different" from his generation. If he draws away from peers, his social skills suffer, and a singer needs great social skills. His sensitivity makes him vulnerable to conflict and frustration in other areas. His talent stems from an intense inner reservoir of perception and passion that can lead to an imbalance of personality structure and stability during his growth and development. He may have overinvolved parents who want him to display his talents. His super-ego or conscience may impose high discipline and expectations on the child.

High achievers, however, having coped with these vicissitudes, are apt to be more robust than the average child, with lower anxiety and a higher drive, one able to take risks, overcoming early triumph or failure.

PLAY

Play is the "work" of childhood, but perhaps if we understand it better we can see why adults still play: play games, give plays (let's pretend), play instruments, and see how something plays a part in something else. Even when a piece of something mechanical is loose, we say it has some "play". Singing also can qualify as play, even when we speak of "serious" music. We play with the timing, the words, even the meaning.

If you look carefully you see child's play is systematic and rule-governed. This must be because while he is growing and developing in the marvelous ways we have noted (pun intended), the child needs to frame his activities as best he can by structures of who, what, when, where, so the growth can be patterned and he continues to learn better who he is, in context. Structured play influences the child to structure his reality with his developing language.

Playful behavior is imaginative, exuberant, enjoyable. While play seems to have no purpose except having "fun", there is a less obvious element when play allows the child to act out how he feels about his experiences. In pretending, the child can express indirectly and over and over not only his pleasures but his fears and worries. Thus he can reexperience them in non-threatening disguises and so gradually master them.

One difference between play and artistry, or professional sports, is that it has no goal and no product, but it does have systematic relations to what is not play. It relates to creativity, problem solving, language learning, as well as to learning social roles. This is why child-play manifests itself in the adult mind, and contributes a depth of meaning to adult musical play.

When play takes the form of improvisation, it has no rules, no wrongs, and it brings a sense of freedom. Play is not a disease, it is a re-creation.

THE COMMUNICATION HABITS OF THE SINGER

All the arts have at least one purpose: to communicate. As speakers and singers, and as teachers and scientists studying and aiding speakers and singers, we need to understand what we can communicate and by what means.

We are not talking here about everyday conversation, nor about journalistic memo-writing, but about the more universal concerns of poetry and music, and therefore about the psychology of the writer, the composer, the actor, the singer, and the audience.

Specifically, we are talking about the adult artist's communicative systems, which are based on this childhood development of communication skills.

We all have shared these crucial childhood developmental experiences, and this growth process has laid down similar patterns in each of our brains and nervous systems. It is basically these meanings of life and growth that we can communicate and that we can understand about each other.

It is these patterned meanings that continue generation after generation to move the creative artist to formulate and express. These are what the interpretive artist subconsciously understands in the poetry and music. These are what the audience members are longing to have expressed to them without their knowing it, and what they can study further in the work.

To see what these shared experiences and growth patterns are we must go back to the formative processes at the beginning of life, and see how these affect the resulting structure of our communication habits. I am much indebted to my husband, Arthur Wormhoudt, for helping me apply his theory of how the early acquired habits explain much of the structure of literature, to shed light on musical and poetical structure and meaning.

The infant gains information both about its self and its world through the senses of touch, hearing, and vision. Smell and taste are operative but less informative. This sequence of tactile, auditory and visual experience makes a three-part pattern, and it is possible this underlies the typical three-part song form, the A-B-A, with the second A enhanced by visual discoveries.

The infant's tactile experience occurs in a 5-stage pattern. He first lies supine; at 5 or 6 months he sits up; then he crawls "on all fours"; toward the end of the first year he very precariously stands upon two feet; and finally he walks—homo sapiens!

These kinesthetic changes are a part of the basis for language, the communication arts of speech and song, writing and reading.

In the supine position the infant coos and cries. Sitting up changes the effect of gravity on his torso, and also changes the feeling of the breathing (so fundamental for the singer). The effect of the gravity and the breathing changes is to break up the cooing stream into smaller articulated parts that eventually become the syllables of the child's native language.

Crawling produces an elation in the ability to move about. The psychological mood has to be less passive, more aggressive. The child can explore his visual world but from a low level. Note also he is now four-footed, feeling movement rhythms in 2's and 4's. (Later, armies march to bands playing in 4/4 time). This very kinesthetic crawling phase helps the child further to differentiate outer world from inner world. This may be the basis for his gaining the two language structures: the stability of semantic relationships, and the movement of syntactical relationships.

In due time muscles and bones and curiosity grow and strengthen, and the child stands up. He is wobbly, but aha! his hands are now free, and it won't be long before he writes scribbling streams, just as he began auditory communication with a babbling stream. And yes, he has gained under-standing.

The next step in this drama is precisely that, he takes his first steps and now walks on two. This triumph of rhythm and balance develops into speaking full words, then sentences and little songs, and eventually becoming the scribe who puts down the symbols.

So in the first months of life we gain information about our new post-natal world, first chiefly through inner kinesthetic and outer tactile experience, then through give and take auditory events, and finally through a more accessible visual world. At the same time we are going through the five-phase kinetic development. Overseeing all of this (and that is a metaphor of inner to outer world) and reacting to it, we have a two-sided brain, our musical brain.

In general, as we saw, the right side processes visual and spatial information, the left side, temporal information and therefore speech.

There is a much wider variation in the location of musical capacities. Howard Gardner, research psychologist at Harvard University, reports that the right side of the brain is important for recognizing pitch and timbre. Sensitivity to rhythm seems to be located in both hemispheres, with the left slightly dominant. Musical training seems to cause the left hemisphere to house more of the musical abilities once housed in the right. This helps explain how a singer puts together right side music and left side words at the same moment.

The study of song literature affords an excellent opportunity to gain insights into the ways in which the two arts of poetry and music enhance each other's meaning. We have said that musical ideas cannot be expressed in words, but to some extent the composer is doing precisely this when he sets a poem to music. The poet who is fortunate enough to have a good composer make a song for his words will have succeeded, in part, in realizing the music of his words.

For the singer who sings the song, these interrelationships are especially important since he cannot communicate the poet's or the composer's intentions unless he understands them.

Before I proceed to an analysis of a particular song to illustrate how I think these interrelationships appear, there are several general principles that should be stated. First, the words of a poem and the notes of a song have their primary reference to the communication habits established in childhood, and a secondary reference to events external to these habits. In this respect they differ from scientific statements which refer primarily to events external to the communication habits and only secondarily to the habits themselves. For example, it is often said that poems and music express feelings while scientific articles describe events that occur in the laboratory or field where most feelings are, as yet, singularly elusive. Communication habits involve a good deal more than feelings, but they are more intimately bound up with inner world feelings than are scientific writings. This distinction between ideas that refer to an inner world of communication habits and those that refer to an external world is very old. It is found in John's Gospel where we read that: "In the beginning was the Word and the Word was God". When you add to this the statement of Jesus that the Kingdom of God is within you, the distinction between inner and outer worlds becomes clear. (Note that the Kingdom of God is an English translation of the Greek words *he basileia tou theou*. Basileia is a feminine noun, therefore Queendom. Theou is the basis for English words such as theology, theory, and theater).

The second general principle which is useful to the singer in analyzing a song is that the communication habits, formed in childhood, contain information which can best be understood from a child's point of view, even though the poet and composer are adults. Here again we remember the words of Jesus, that tell us that if we want to enter the Kingdom of God's world we must become as little children.

Modern psychology since Freud has massively documented the ways in which childhood experience forms the foundation for adult behavior. The song which Brahms wrote for the poem of Klaus Groth which I will presently analyze makes an explicit reference to this principle.

A third general principle is, as we have seen, that the communication habits develop in childhood in stages, which the adult poet and composer can represent in the parts of his poem and music.

An examination of Brahms' song Heimweh II: "O wüsst ich doch den Weg zurück" ("Oh, knew I but the way back to childhood's land), shows that he had some kind of a three-part pattern in mind when he chose the poem of Klaus Groth. The poem has four stanzas but Brahms combines the middle two stan-

zas to make a middle section. He does this by using a contrast-
ing tempo, by changing the style of accompaniment, and by using
the same melody for both verses.

' Groth himself gave Brahms a hint for this by making the
rhyme scheme for stanzas one and four identical, whereas the
rhymes for the middle two differ. Brahms repeats part of the last
line in stanzas one and four and emphasizes this with a measure
of 9/4 time which contrasts with the original 6/4. The last lines of
the middle two stanzas, however, are both repeated in their en-
tirety and with no change in the time signal. The all-over 3-part
structure is felt in the choice of 6/4 time.

Turning now to the words of the first stanza or first third of the
pattern, we find the singer expressing the wish to know the way
to return to the land of childhood. In terms of the poet's and
composer's ability to create symbolically, this might be restated
as a desire to recall those memories of childhood experience
when the communication habits were first established.

That they are tactile (walking) habits is implied in the idea
that childhood is a geographical place, *Kinderland,* and in the
idea that one might travel there on a path, *den Weg.* The steadily
proceeding 8th notes in the accompaniment echo this feeling of
feet on the path, and the rise and fall give a searching feeling.

The importance of these early tactile experiences is further
made clear when the singer says that he let go of the mother's
hand and went to seek *dem Glück,* happiness, which is something different from what mother's hand could give. This agrees
with D.W.Winnecott's idea of the good-enough mother.

The mother is a kind of Muse image whose hand holds the
poet's and composer's pen as they write words and notes. As
adults they have had to let go of the hand at times in search of
the happiness that is tied to the need to find food and shelter.
One cannot be happy if one is starving or is cold and wet. But the
need to compose poems and songs is also a compelling need to
which one must return if he is endowed with the ability to satisfy it.

In the second stanza the singer emphasizes that the search

for happiness gives one little time to rest. One is often awakened to struggle for it, and one longs to have his tired eyes closed as he is tucked in bed by loving hands. The search for happiness involves seeking (*forschen*, compare *die Forschung* or scientific research) and leaves little time for dreaming. And dreams are often related to the work of the poet and musician since they show the mind at work when the external senses are cut off from the world outside.

The contrast between the child as a dreamer and the adult as a striver for external goals can best be understood in terms of the development of auditory experience which is built on the foundation of the tactile communication habits. As the infant moves from the immobile sitting position to the crawling position, it learns what it means to exert its leg muscles in an active way. This new sense of movement is appropriate to the development of speech which has a kinetic quality that is different from the child's perception of touch and vision.

Brahms shows this kinetic quality by changing and speeding up the tempo of the middle section. A more complex auditory experience is reflected in the chords of the accompaniment as contrasted with the single 8th notes of the first part.

At the same time the poem contrasts adult and childlike sleep and dreams. This is another hint of the auditory communication habits. Sleep usually occurs at night and this is the time when the external world cannot easily be perceived through touch or vision. But auditory experiences of the external world are just as available as they are in daylight. Brahms hints at the importance of adult daylight experience in the middle third by putting the first measure and a half of the second stanza wholly in the bright treble clef. After this the bass clef returns and is never abandoned. The passage of time which is so much more strongly felt in adulthood than in childhood is also part of the kinetic auditory experience but it is balanced by the second childhood which is possible in dreams, poems, and music.

The last stanza at first seems like a repetition of the first.

However, the visual communication habits are expressed here by the visualization of a second person to whom the singer addresses his request. This second person is the mother or Muse who was mentioned in the first stanza, and hinted at in the second where the poet talked of love tucking the weary child in its bed. Now the Muse is commanded to show the poet and composer the way back to Kinderland. It is no longer a matter of wishing to know the way without any definite idea as to how the wish can be fulfilled. If the Muse is commanded she will presumably be able to fulfill the command. Note the visual word *show*.

So when the singer says: *In vain do I seek for happiness*, he is not merely repeating what he said in line 3 of the first stanza. The tense of the verb has now changed from past to present. The Muse has done her duty and so it is vain to ask her to do more. The way to Kinderland has been traversed by the completion of the poem, and by Brahms' writing down the notes of the last third, very subtly using elements from the accompaniments of the first two parts. By diminishing the 6th scale step on the word *öder Strand (empty* and deserted shore) in contrast to the first verse melody which he keeps in the major key, he expresses the adult nostalgia that his past is past.

The poet and composer may assume that the path is visible before them, and before the singer and the public who hear or read the song. That is, it is visible if the song is a success and the public continues to keep it in the repertory. This is true when the information about the communication habits given by the poem and the song (so far) is sufficient to stimulate the public to further communication. The song helps them do what they could not do spontaneously as the poet and composer did. They now realize they are not only listeners but readers, because the poet and composer were writers, not only speakers and singers.

This shift to the power and permanence of visual communication is especially apparent in the last line, where the rhyme word becomes *Strand* instead of *Hand* which we might not expect since the rhymes in the first and last stanzas are identical not only in sound but in word. We now realize that the geographical setting of the poem is not Kinderland but the North Sea coast which Brahms knew in his boyhood in Hamburg. Groth also grew up in North Germany and wrote some of his poems in the Plattdeutsch of the coastal regions. The empty beach that surrounds the singer thus contains traces of the summer crowds who came here to enjoy the cool bathing and escape from heat at these famous resort areas.

What the singer sees is what Longfellow makes his observer see at the end of the *Psalm of Life*: "footprints on the sands of time". There is a note of sadness in this deserted place, but there is also a satisfaction in knowing that what one has written has made some kind of imprint, however fleeting. As the child shifts from the crawling phase to the two-footed walking which symbolizes adult behavior, he realizes with regret that he no longer has the full muscular power of a four-footed animal. But upright posture brings with it a new kind of vision. The beach surrounds, *ringsum*, the way the hand grasps the pen, and this brings with it a new kind of power.

Brahms places the accompaniment for the last three measures in the bass clef to suggest the adult vision which has been attained. This contrasts with the child's resurrection theme in the middle third where the treble clef introduced the second stanza. On the other hand the presence of the North Sea is a reminder of the prenatal bliss which the child lost at birth.

It should be clear that the conclusion of the song is highly complex. It is not mere grief at the loss of childhood nor is it a simple praise of the Muse.

To recapitulate, we have 2-part patterns in our two brain halves, and in our bi-pedal balance and locomotion. A 3-part pattern results from the development sequence of tactile, auditory and visual perceptions. These 3-parts are congruent with 1st, 3rd, and 5th phases of the 5-part kinetic development. These childhood phases of growth and development lay down the basis of our communication habits, and they come to fruition in the works of the adult artist and scientist.

Our languages are wise. We say we "understand" something. We say we "grasp" an idea. We say "I see what you mean". Our scientists may feel the "gravity" of a situation and therefore "weigh" the evidence. And then, the Muse gives us our museums and music itself.

This, incidentally, leads to an aesthetic point regarding the best performer for our Brahms song. A woman's voice will call up the feminine Muse, and a high woman's voice will also echo the child in Kinderland. Elly Ameling has sung this to perfection. The song is equally fine in a lower man's voice, since this feels like Brahms' voice speaking, and emphasizes the work of the mature artist.

So there are some individuals with a strong leaning toward auditory expression. Some become professional speakers. Some become singers, who communicate through song, which among other things is an echo of Kinderland.

—Everything we can do, we learned as a technique while we were children.

—Wesley Balk

—The great man is he who does not lose his childhood.

—Mencius

—To sing, be like a child.

—Benita Valente

—Insofar as an artist is an artist, he remains a child. Once he grows up, all is lost.

—Ned Rorem

CHAPTER IV

Sometimes I Feel Like a Motherless Child
or I Think I Can, I Think I Can

THE ADOLESCENT SINGER

These musical children we have been studying in Chapter III then enter puberty and their 12 to 20 adolescent years. At this point I feel a bit like Lewis Carroll's White Rabbit, who asked "Where shall I begin?" The King replied "Begin at the beginning and go on till you come to the end, and then stop".

PSYCHOLOGY IN A VOICE LESSON

Since singers usually begin voice lessons or performing as teenagers, let us begin by looking at what happens psychologically in a typical voice lesson. I will write this from the teacher's point of view, and after that we can take up the nature of adolescent growth, and then how the individual works to combine personal and musical development.

Singing is a potent art, communicating through three media: the poetry, the music, and the singer. First the poet communicates through his poetry. The composer responds to these structures and meanings, not merely translating these into written music, but communicating further through his musical structures. The singer responds to both structures by converting these into sounds through his vocal instrument, and so re-embodies what the poet has written on the page and the composer has notated on the score. He communicates to a listener. If the communication is successful, listeners respond in appropriate ways to keep the song alive as a communicating vehicle.

The poetic and musical structure, the singer's interpretation of these, and the audience's appreciation of the meanings are all based on childhood patterns of development. As I have outlined in the last chapter, this early development of communication habits underlies the psychology of the adult situation of learning to sing, teaching singing, and performing.

Singers make song based on their physiology, physics, and psychology. Teachers of singers operate on their knowledge of psychology, vocal physiology, and physics.

Singing is, above all, a way of communicating. It is one mind using its vocal instrument to convey information, ideas, relationships, feelings about both inner and outer worlds, to other minds.

Important as the physical aspects of tone production are, the psychology of the effort plays an equally important part. Herein lie the reasons for singing at all, for the message being conveyed, for the singer's dynamism and the audience's reception.

To see how extensive are the psychological aspects of singing, let us walk through a typical voice lesson. We will stop the action whenever we need to think about how the psyche is involved.

The student arrives at your studio door. STOP. The fact that he comes in reminds us that he has in his mind a long-range and a short-term motivation. Long-range is his dream/concept of the better singer-performer he wants to become, and the strength of that motivation will affect all of his technical and artistic work. Short-term, he has some notion of where he is in this development, and what it is he wants or needs from this lesson. The teacher will also have long and short goals for this singer. It is the teacher's duty to bring all four of these motives into acceptable working order, each lesson or series of lessons.

You and the student greet each other. STOP. The student, however far off in his own world he may seem, reads your manner and tone of voice to know how interested and eager you are to work with him today. This will affect how trusting he will be in his efforts. You in turn will gather information which helps determine the handling of this lesson: the student's general and vocal health, whether tired or rested, whether stressed or relaxed. Here is a prime example of one on one psychological transaction.

The lesson begins with the first vocalise, which will serve as not only physiological and physical-acoustic training, but also psychological purposes such as the assurance gained in the freeing process, the release of stress or tension, the pleasure and further motivation gained by controlling and coordinating the instrument in a successful exercise. And above all, the student's sufficient understanding of the relation of what he is asked to do to one or more of the four motives first described.

So the student breathes and opens his mouth to make the first sound. STOP. To make any sound louder or more emphatic than normal speech, he must gather his courage to break the silence. The psychological atmosphere of the studio can encourage him to lose fear. It can also instill more fear.

But with courage the student blows the given pitches and vowels. STOP. In fact, three STOPS. The first concerns the ease and balance of his breathing. If he is giving up old incorrect tensions he may temporarily feel out of muscular control, which is a physical-psychological feeling he must understand. Second, he may worry so much about being on pitch that he manufactures notes and forgets to think the phrase. He must have the experience that pitch is far more a mental than a physical skill and that his brain will give it to him if he doesn't stop to worry. And third, if his vowels are not clear and resonant, he must endure quite a period of having the heritage of his personal diction invaded.

He sings the first vocalise and you both monitor it. STOP. We are now not only in the realm of physics which determines the character of the acoustic production, but in the realm of psycho-acoustics: how we hear and how our brain interprets the hearing. You will modify what you ask of the student by your understanding of the nature of this objective-subjective auditory experience. The student, in turn, learns to rely on your ears when he realizes his perception is different than that of his hearers.

Now you can offer more vocalises, meeting all the criteria for the first one and in addition choosing them in the light of needs shown by the production of the preceding exercise. The choice, and its method of presentation, has to be based on some theory of the learning process. Our educational psychology must relate to this *singing* learning process.

Surely the lesson can now progress without quite so much mental sweat. Our goals (motives) are fairly clear and fairly close together, you each have established a trust in each other, the worst inhibitions are overcome, the need for change and the resulting new integrated mind/body coordination is accepted, you can make allowance for psycho-acoustic phenomena, and you have a plan for the most efficient teaching/learning process.

Fine. Due to the progress made, the student's work on the vocalises has been exciting to you both, a psychological response, and now he can put all that good technique into a song. STOP, just long enough to realize that the brain is structurally divided into right and left brain. Words are processed in the left, whereas music is at first heard in the right brain. To sing poems, the singer must bring together these two memory banks.

The accompaniment begins, but STOP. The singer is about to communicate, and the technique is there only to serve that art. He must then communicate through the poetry and the music and his vocal tone and his body expression. So his mind must be well-stocked with well-studied meanings that can then be expressed through these media. The most fundamental meanings stem from the poetry, which in turn stem from those communication habits established in childhood. We may well say with Brahms and Klaus Groth "O, if I only knew the lovely way back to childhood's land". Words are metaphors giving access to childhood foundations in phrases such as "the song *flows* smoothly", and "on *wings* of song". Childhood development, through stages of sensory experience and growth, establishes mental (psychological) patterns that result in the forms and expressive meanings of all art. Now the accompaniment may continue, when the singer has a grasp of the patterns and meanings in the poetry and in the composer's enhancement of these.

If we leave out all the gentle housekeeping that has to be done on both the technique and artistry shown in singing the song, the lesson is finished.

Now for the performance on stage:

The singer makes his entrance with his accompanist, and recognizes his audience. STOP. Body handling, facial expression, and dress all send messages before the poetry, music, and voice have a chance. Let's not give the audience psychological indigestion by having the first set of messages incompatible with the second.

Quiet now, for the first song. STOP. Stage fright? Mental panic? Knees quivering? Heart racing? Breathing shallow? Not the best situation for being in mental control of all facets of the hoped-for artistic message. But not to worry, the teacher and the student have foreseen this hazard, analyzed the psychological causes and practiced solutions, and so shortly the singer is in command of himself. Paola Novikova told me "The first song is always for the singer, to establish himself".

The singer is in control of his performance attitude, his body, and his technique, but STOP. His memory has failed. Well, he coolly fakes through a few un-dictioned words or improvised rhythms. However, a good deal of evidence has been gathered on how we memorize, and we may find better ways of retrieving the total message from the memory.

With everything back in hand, the singer can put the instrument on cruise drive and enter the thorny fields of "interpretation". He has already given this much thought while learning the song, but on stage nothing can be mechanical. Such a rote performance sends the wrong message. This kind of "winging" it is not well grounded. His "interpretation" is actually not a lot of his own ideas put into whipped cream on top of the composer's and poet's ideas. It is essentially his thorough involvement in, understanding of, and service to the music and poetry. All the message is contained in the song, in his instrument singing that song, and in his understanding of both the song and the instrument. The sung message comes from a sensitive psyche using a disciplined instrument.

As Adriana Lecouvreur sings: "Io son l'umile ancella del genio creator". "I am the humble servant of the creative genius". The art lies in the work of understanding and of imagination. But to say that does not explain it. We need more understanding of our understanding.

One more STOP before the singer continues his recital. If the purpose of singing is an intense kind of communication, the singer needs his audience. To hit the mark, he needs to give thought to these listeners' psychological needs, or he is wasting his time and theirs. What can he sing, and how can he sing it, that will be true to the "genio creator" and at the same time meet some communicative needs of his audience? We speak much of the freeing of the voice. This is precisely one of the gifts of a good singer to his audience: the freedom of that soaring sound.

Having swiftly decided on some solution to each of these psychological activities as the need arose, we have gotten through a lesson, then a performance. Now let us summarize what these activities are.

The first aspect is that of motivation. We may never know precisely why we want to be a singer, but certain reasons and goals can be ascertained and strengthened.

Secondly, there is the learning process of building the instrument. The more we know about this the faster the student's mind will be in charge of a disciplined instrument.

The third aspect is an equally big task, to understand the

psychological meanings in the poem, the music, and the performance, all of which are based on the childhood development of communication habits.

The fourth area is that of psycho-acoustics, how the brain interprets what it hears.

Fifth and last, are the psychological challenges of performance, which can make or break a singer even after the first four aspects are mastered.

My purpose here is to suggest a framework for thinking about the psychological aspects of our work as singers and teachers of singers. It is my hope that we can further clarify what we know and what we do not know about these aspects, so that we can build and share an accurate, useful, detailed psychology of singing and teaching singing.

ADOLESCENT GROWTH PATTERNS

Puberty begins with the hormonal happening, which has strong effects on the young mind, young body, and noticeably on the young voice. Growth will proceed along four lines: the inner biological, the personal psychological, the outer physical, and the sociological cultural. These do not work out in synchrony, so the young person is pretty busy keeping up with and adding together all these new growths. Some floundering in handling them is to be expected.

Adolescence is, however, a developmental stage that offers great, even exciting, opportunities for growth and positive outcomes. College freshmen, leaving the structured life of home, grow into greater autonomy. They make plans for the future and develop close relationships in both inter-personal and work related activities. Issues they confront are loneliness, roommate problems, freedom from supervision, response to drugs and alcohol, sexuality, value conflicts, money management and cultural diversity. This is no small task, and beginning to find one's true voice can be a thrilling way to finding one's true self, bravely coping.

The big questions begin to come up—who am I? and who do I want to be? What am I doing here? And for the singer: Will I be a good-enough singer? (Does anybody care about me?)

The teacher needs to relate the learning process to the emotional maturity of the student, and to his goals. This is why I always ask at the first lesson, why he wants lessons, what use he will be making of his singing voice, and what help he thinks he needs. Every step of the building process involves a new discipline for the student, and just how far the teacher can insist on this depends on the emotional maturity. The student has to be willing to give up more immediate goals for a longer-range discipline that cannot be accomplished all at once.

D.W.Winnicott says growing up means taking the parent's place. "In the unconscious fantasy, growing up is inherently an aggressive act. And the child is no longer child size". The teenager is saying "I exist, in my own right". Unconscious fantasy underlies playing, and it also underlies the aggression that fuels teen-ager rebellions. This ambiguous position of aggression/vulnerability may make the singer feel and act shy. This can interfere with producing louder vocal sounds, especially by young women. They may be afraid that loudness is aggressive, when actually the aggression is expressed by withholding voice. Getting some girls to sing out easily is one of the most confounding tasks for a teacher. This kind of soft singing is a passive solution to handling aggressive feelings, and "excuse-me" passivity never made a free singer.

There is another reason for the girl's breathy voice. When we speak of the hormonal effect of the changing voice in puberty, we are usually thinking of the boy's voice, since that change is more dramatic and noticeable in him than in a girl. However, the girl's voice does change. The instrument grows a bit larger and will develop a "chest" register in addition to adding strength to the child's high voice. At this point for a while, many girls will have a breathy sound, which also makes it softer. This is a growth and technical matter which will be changed by further maturation and by tuning the vocal tract to find the clear vowel resonance. The student's psychological confidence can be boosted by the teacher's explaining the acoustics of vowel formation. This can be done briefly, clearly, and with this new understanding of how her instrument works, she will be quite willing to clarify her vowel concepts and find the resonance track. The excitement of finding the first clear easily produced vowels will greatly increase her motivation for maintaining this level of clear un-breathy sound.

If one vowel/pitch in a song phrase gives trouble, it helps to vocalize the pair of front or back vowels which are most resonant on that pitch. Then pair the most resonant vowels with the vowel/pitch giving trouble. This modifies the needed vowel toward clarity and resonance just enough to make it the correct vowel, surprisingly. After a while this setting of the instrument by the mind's clear vowel concept becomes automatic. I have found the vocalises in Berton Coffin's book *Overtones of Bel Canto*, based on the most resonant vowels on a pitch, to be of tremendous help in the student's gaining this new understanding. The most resonant vowel pairs on a given pitch are to be found in the chart accompanying Coffin's book.

The teen age boy doesn't ordinarily have this breathy transition from child to adult voice. However, through this changing voice period, he will also need explanation and motivation. He usually will not be taking voice lessons until the voice settles, which gives the Junior High choral director the responsibility and the pleasure of helping him keep going and growing. The teacher needs to know for both boys and girls how to create a desire to sing through this development, how to increase the ability to sing, and above all safeguard the health of the growing vocal mechanism.

For singers the experiences in Junior High will almost make or break the ability and pleasure they will have in singing well. Blessed be the teachers who guide them. Motivation is the first concern, because the boy or girl may not have had any past instruction, may be afraid to sing in a room full of strangers, or may dislike the music. Desire, helpful training, and practice will get them through this growing period. They must understand what is happening, that *all* the voices in their group are maturing, and get the feeling that "singers come through". It will help to work on music that does not demand extremes in vocal range and dynamics, but is challenging and appealing to them.

SELF-IDENTITY, SELF-MANAGEMENT, SELF-ESTEEM

Defining the self and strengthening its integration is the main work of these years. It is a process of making real one's potential through one's own efforts. It is not a static goal toward which individuals strive consciously or unconsciously. It is a process, an ever ongoing activity, toward a changing goal. Self-esteem grows from achievement, supportive praise, and belonging to a group.

There are three ways of thinking about the self, or three selves. Our *actual* self is the sum of our individual experience. There is the *real* self that is responsible for integrating self parts harmoniously. Then there is the *ideal* self. If the expectations in this self are unrealistically high, the result can be self-hatred when these are not reached.

Inner "theater scripts" have been written by early childhood experiences that have a lasting effect on the adolescent and the adult mind. These scripts underlie much of the adolescent's attitudes and behaviors. Such highly emotional preverbal traumas, with no words to define them, add confusion during a teen's growth. The body then acts on the mind's distress. That is, if it seems too dangerous to symbolize one's problem in language, then the psyche's primitive message is expressed by the body in various symptoms. When this happens, there are no words to connect the physical distress to its mind/body emotional base. Every time such un-named feelings are called up, the adolescent grows if he/she copes well with it. It helps to have someone to talk to, or even just one who is sympathetic without speaking of any difficulty—this can be a peer, a parent, a teacher or adult mentor. There is in the teen-ager a yearning for clarity and for structure.

One way of coping is to sing, for the music and the words can express some of the unknown situation and the singer's growth of controlling it. The more the singer is in control of his feelings, the more expressive he can be. This, of course, is far from being the only motivation for singing.

Finding one's identity is also not the only work of adolescence, but let's see what is involved in this part. Michael Eigen, in his book, *The Electric Tightrope*, points out that when we breathe in a supply of more air than we actually need, it gives us a feeling of well-being. So the singer has a psychological as well as a technical reason for being at ease and adept in breath-taking. Keep in mind, too, that the teenager's breathing is still immature. Steady breathing is one experience that Eigen believes helps identify the self in the midst of the fluctuation happening in many other adolescent experiences.

If one can begin to identify oneself, it is then possible to improve in self-management. This is a difficult part of adolescent growth, so that management of thoughts and behavior can be for a time much too loose (not enough control, witness many a teenager's room), or much too tight (so that spontaneity is lost). In each case anxiety can rise. For the singer, the clarity of at least partial answers to the questions "Who am I?" and "What am I doing?" can encourage his organizing a sleeping-eating-study-practice-performance-play schedule that is reasonable and aims toward the goals of physical health, psychological autonomy, and artistic growth.

Herman Hesse, in *Steppenwolf*, says: one, therefore "who gets so far as making the supposed unity of the self twofold is already almost a genius, in any case a most exceptional person". Every ego is far from being a unity. It is a collection of forms, of stages, of inheritance, of potentialities, all to be melded into a challenged self.

If the singer has negative thoughts: "It doesn't sound good", or "I'm not making progress", his self-confidence cannot be strong. Gradually he must learn to think: "I can sing", "I can improve", "I like myself", "I like my sound".

Attainment of some positive self-identity and self-management, along with a positive body image, are what builds self-esteem. This growth is an absolute necessity for a singer, for a weak self-esteem leaves one feeling very vulnerable and full of anxiety. A strong self-esteem allows one to go onstage and share courage, understanding, and freedom to be, with an audience.

Part of this strength comes from gaining a favorable body image. In the gender stereotype, for the boy this means "strong", for the girl it means "thin". When the belief of being "strong" or "thin" is not maintained by the adolescent, the negative feelings about his/her appearance kill any performing pleasure he/she might have. This is true even when realistically the body is normal and the adolescent only thinks it is not.

The body image is distorted by irrational thoughts, unrealistic expectations, faulty explanations. There are several rules that cause dysfunctional concepts:

(1) Misinterpreting outside events so as to see a personal reference when there is none,
(2) Polarized thinking, seeing events in extremes of good or bad,
(3) Jumping to conclusions when evidence is lacking. These cognitive errors must be overcome to gain true self-esteem.

Underlying performance anxiety is a lack of self-esteem. Underlying lack of self-esteem is a negative body image. Or to put this in the developmental sequence: a negative body image underlies lack of self-esteem, then lack of self-esteem underlies performance anxiety. More of this in Chapter VI.

ADOLESCENT MATURATION

This growth out of immaturity into a mature adult is slow, allowing time for the marshalling of forces, the facing of various challenges, the coping with success or temporary defeat. Those children who for any reason (a parent's death, divorce, financial crises) are forced early into assuming adult maturity will not have stored up the strength of the longer growth pattern. The work that thus has been skipped over will have to be done at some later age.

Good things also are working due to the teen-ager's immaturity. He is not "set in his ways". In traversing new mental/physical ground he can have creative thoughts and activities relative to his situation. He will experience new feelings, have new insights both about himself and his environment, dream new dreams for his future. And sing new songs.

The slow maturation of the voice is the teen-ager's situation. Would a flutist or a trumpeter feel really sure of himself if his instrument made continuous changes over several years? This means that the singer must understand how his voice will mature, so that as his voice improves he can feel that the maturation process is working for him, not against him.

It is not only that maturation brings new feelings in the vocal instrument, but the sound also changes. One large factor in our identity is how our voice sounds, so that if the sound changes it may feel as though part of the self is drifting away. This is where the teacher needs to help the singer understand that this new sound is revealing the true self, not losing it. Hundreds of times I have had a student break through to a more vibrant, more free sound, after which he would make a face and say, in effect, "Oh, that's a bad sound". The best immediate remedy I have found is to have the singer place two large song albums at right angles to the head in front of each ear, and repeat the way he just sang. This is a gimmick, but it allows him to hear himself a little more "off the walls", and he is truly surprised to find how good that sounds. This, in my experience, is a red-letter day. Finally, he knows how to gain a resonance, and knows that every time he does, the tone will seem easy and strong. Once the sound of healthy technique is accepted. he can pay far more attention to the expressive use. Both student and teacher must keep in mind this voice has changed from a child voice but is not yet mature.

THE NEED FOR ACCEPTANCE—NEW RELATIONSHIPS

Not only must the adolescent gain a new and stronger sense of self, he needs to find some acceptance from his peers while he gains more independence from his parents. These are challenges that many teens will meet quite well. Others may have some difficulty and a few will take a tumultuous course.

If a singer feels too "different", he will act different and perhaps his peers will feel put off. This can be a crucial time when the singer/performer may try to connect with a group by smoking or drinking or otherwise acting out. The singer may then ask "is singing worth while?" A teacher or counselor may help him see that he can gain more confidence in his whole self, not just his singer-self, and so find other ways of connecting with peers, perhaps in art or drama or sports.

Two things are working at once in normal mid-adolescence. There is a need to diminish the dependence on the parents and therefore a need to reach out to a peer or a group in the environment, who are called by psychiatrists "transitional objects". These attachments help maintain some balance during all the biological, physical, and cognitive changes taking place. The changes disrupt the childhood sense of self, so the adolescent is forced to reorganize the core sense of who he is, and must develop new self-regulating functions. Old ideals and models are abandoned, and psycho-social demands to separate from family are felt. This means trying to find an independent place in the world, while feeling pressures also to engage in sexual and emotional intimacy. Efrain Bleiberg says that when adolescents disengage from the internalized parents, their new self-regulating capacities help them see their parents as reality interpreters and general supporters of their children's growth.

In childhood, the adolescent has felt omnipotent. In this transitional position, he can call up this attitude to deny feelings of vulnerability and incompetence. Bleiberg points out that this disowned experience of weakness or failure can be projected on parents or other adults, and further, that at this point self-esteem becomes contingent on peer approval. This may be reflected in a way of dressing, a kind of music liked, or use of a certain vocabulary with special meaning.

It is obvious that all this impinges on what the singer wants to sing and how he wants to sing it. As this new growth progresses, there will be a strong chance for a broad and deep musical interest to develp. This further motivates the singer to explore his new capabilities and an enticing new repertoire. The growth is toward a realistic and challenging outlook.

DICTION

The situation of feeling some loss of self also occurs when clarifying diction. In speech all kinds of pitch slips and slides happen, and extra vowels are sounded or omitted, and often the worst diction and thus the worst tonality occurs in one's native language. But one's diction is what one grew up with, and therefore is part of one's self-image. To be more plain with vowels and consonants means changing that early diction sound, and again self-identity is threatened. However, when the clearer diction is gained, the resulting clarity of resonance and meaning contributes to a new, more ideal, self.

This clinging to early speech habits can carry over into professional life. When Samuel Barber's *Anthony and Cleopaatra* opera was commissioned to open the new Metropolitan Opera House, tenors were auditioned for the role of Anthony. Nicolai

Gedda was chosen over American tenors, partly for the convincing clarity of his English diction.

NON-ACCEPTANCE OF PRAISE

Lowered self-esteem may have another consequence, that the singer cannot tolerate being praised. If singers cannot accept rewards, it is because they see the reward as a matter of luck or just chance, not due to the fact that their own action is praiseworthy. This non-acceptance is worse in relation to the teacher, who wants to praise whatever the singer does that deserves praise, in order to alert the student to what he is doing right. But if the student feels his work falls so short of what he thinks is good (and this is the tendency for the learning singer), he simply cannot accept that praise as being true.

The long-term solution for the student to be able to accept his due is for the teacher to always be perfectly honest—to say what is good (and the praise need not be higher than "good"), and never to praise something that is not good. The student thus learns to trust the teacher because she means what she says, and she is supposed to have good ears. If the singer trusts that the good parts are indeed good, he will all the sooner bring the not-good parts in line, and so raise his belief in himself and in his voice.

It is just as necessary for the teacher not to point out directly what sounds the student is making that tell her or him what the student is doing wrong. Once, one of my young men said, at a moment of curiosity and not understanding: "You are often telling me 'good'. Why don't you ever say 'bad'"? "Well", I replied, "do you notice that when I don't say 'good', I do suggest trying another way of making those sounds?" Often a very simple modification of the effort makes the difference.

MOTIVATION

We have seen how a negative self-image breaks down the

singer's feeling of having something to give. Conversely, a positive self-image will work for the student to be more motivated toward learning and giving. This is the age when moral questions arise, particularly in connection with relationships—new relations to family, and new loyalties to peers. Morality also brings a sense of needing to contribute to the welfare of one's community, and this causes the singer to feel more giving of his talent.

The singer's motivation is important because it furnishes at least a 20% share in his musical interest and achievements, otherwise fueled by his intelligence, aptitude, and socio-economic background. These last factors, as pointed out by Edward Asmus, are hardly under the voice teacher's control, but the teacher can helpfully manipulate the motivation. If the teacher can offer interesting and clear goals, the student will want to learn the necessary skills, and will participate in music learning activities. The voice teacher or the choral director has the use of a great motivator: the song literature. Finding and picking the best songs for the student and his situation is crucial. As the student reaches each step toward his goal, his motivation continues to be spurred.

Occasionally a student will fail to meet the desired goal. The teacher needs to help him understand this too is a part of learning, that as in golf not every putt goes in the hole. The student can be helped to analyze what went wrong, and together they can figure out what to do about it. This base of understanding a shortcoming and imagining how to change for the better will be an absolute need in a professional singer's career. The fact is the more control the student has over his lesson's work, with of course his teacher's guidance, the better he will understand his achievements, and the more motivated he will be to sing well. The student has a need to be confident and self-determining. Let him, when he feels he is coming short, dare to go back to depending on his wonderful mind and beautiful mind/body abilities, to trust them and let them do his work. This I define as "care-less".

Lucky is the singer who because of childhood and elementary and secondary school experiences has learned an attitude of great interest in music. This attitude is closely related to the self-concept in musical achievement. This child can stand and sing.

Edward Asmus has set up a model of achievement motivation in music. He found that students attribute musical achievement to effort, musical ability, emotional interest in music, classroom environment, and their own background experience. Studies also show that positive self-concept, self-efficiency, self-determination are the perceptions of self that, together with the attributions just listed aid in a focus on the music learning task. Factors extrinsic to the student that weigh on the task are music materials, teaching strategies, and social value. The student's focus on the task brings achievement. This successful outcome also leads to feedback into the start of the system, bringing more attributions and self-perceptions to contribute energy to the next music learning task.

MUSICIANS' PERSONALITY

We have some data on how all this growth of a genetic organism in a family/societal environment can result in a person wanting to be a singer. To focus on this let us first look at what are possible general personal characteristics, in order better to appreciate those that are true of musicians, and particularly of singers.

The Myers-Briggs Type Indicator (MBTI) is based on psychiatrist Carl Jung's theories about universal human mental processes. It begins with four pairs of opposite kinds of functioning:

> *Introversion-Extroversion (I-E)*—the first describes those who pay more attention to their inner world of concepts and ideas, and the second refers to those who focus on their outer world of people and things,

Sensing-Intuition (S-N)—the process of perception, based either on sensory messages or subconscious insight,

Thinking-Feeling (T-F)—the function of judgment, the first being logical and objective, the second being judgment based on personal values.

Judging-Perceiving (J-P)—refers to the attitude people take to the outer world, so the first will use one of the thinking or feeling judgmental processes, the second will not have a judgmental attitude.

The personality will be determined by whichever side of each pair is the stronger. If you are a sensing type, and your thinking is generally stronger than feeling, you can be ISTJ or ISTP, ESTP, or ESTJ. If feeling is stronger, you may be ISFJ, ISFP, ESFP, or ESFJ.

If, however, you operate more on intuition (N) than sensing, but also your feeling about your situation is generally stronger than your thinking, you may be INFJ, or INFP, or INTF or ENTF. Or, finally, if you are more intuitive than sensing, but thinking is stronger than feeling, you are INTJ, or INTF, or ENTF, or ENTJ. Altogether, these clusters outline a possible sixteen personality types.

For example, an ISTJ person will be quiet, serious, practical, organized, and working steadily toward his own established goals. An ISFJ person will also be a quiet sort, friendly, responsible, and concerned with how others feel. The person who is perceptive rather than judging (ISFP), will also be quiet and friendly, but does not care to lead and so will be a loyal follower, and being less judgmental (decision-making) will enjoy the present moment.

When the personality falls on the extrovert side, an ESFP will be outgoing, accepting (not judging), will like sports and making things, have common sense, and ability with both people and things.

If the extroverted persons are more judging than perceiving (ESFJ), they are born cooperators, warm-hearted, talkative, doing things for others, and they work harder if praised. The extrovert who bases decisions on thinking rather than feeling (ESTJ), will be quite realistic and with a definite interest in business or mechanics. These persons like to run activities, but to do well they must remember to take into account other people's feelings. An ESTP person is the 8th of the sensing types, who is also realistic, matter of fact, and sometimes blunt, works best with real things and avoids long explanations.

If we turn from these sensing types to the intuitives, there will again be eight personalities, four stronger in feeling and four stronger in thinking. The INFJ are firm characters, with a strong desire to do well in their own work or for others. They are generally respected and honored for leading others to see how to serve the common good. INTJ persons have a strong drive mainly for their own purposes. Their original minds are critical and independent. The thinking but more perceiving than judging individual (INTP) is reserved and quiet, with much ability in theoretical or scientific subjects, little ability for small talk but much interested in ideas. The INFP person will also care about ideas, and learning and language, and will tend to get more done than looks possible. They are friendly but absorbed in what they are doing.

The extrovert who is also intuitive and works from feeling and perceiving (ENFP) is warm, enthusiastic, quick to see solutions and willing to help anybody with a problem. This person can improvise much in responses instead of preparing ahead of time. The ENTP person is also quick, good company, problem-solving but may not take care of routine work, and turns from one new interest to another. If the person acts more on judgment than perception (ENTJ), he is a good student, a leader in activities, good at reasoning and speaking, but his inner life is more intuitive than sensing. Finally, an ENFJ is very strong in the combination of intuition and feeling and so is sensitive to other's feelings and is sociable and popular. Intuition looks at patterns underlying surface facts, and feeling encourages the use of intuition. These persons will be happiest in work that involves the unfolding of possibilities.

None of these categories fit perfectly, but it does appear, according to Jung and subsequent studies, that the difference in people's personalities results from whether they focus most attention on their inner or outer world, from the way they prefer to take in information (sensing or intuiting), whether they make decisions on the basis of thinking or feeling, and whether they orient themselves to the external world by judging or perceiving.

It is very possible that whatever personality a child is developing may not be valued in its environment, so that the child will try to manage by damping down that part of self-function that is not as acceptable. This will certainly cause some difficulty in the growth of adolescent self-esteem, but the long-term personality will not be affected. This problem will occur more often to more introverted children, who may seem stupid or rebellious or less interested in activities. Antonio Damasio says that the way emotions are utilized is very important in the formation of personality and of conscience, and emotional interest drives the learning process.

Now we can turn to what has been learned about a musician's personality. The first question is, does the personality cause the attraction to music, or does studying music affect the personality? Anthony Kemp believes the first answer is true, that a certain personality and temperament is attracted to the study of music. Kemp's studies found that introversion is a stable factor in performing musicians, and that a link exists between introversion and the interpretational aspects of musical performance. He also found evidence that there was a certain link in temperament between "those involved in the interpretation and performance of music and those who composed it in the first place". The association between the MBTI characteristics of Intuition (N) and Feeling (F) and the process of creativity appears to be quite strong.

When Kemp compared music teachers to performers, he found a higher level of extroversion in the teachers, compared to the high level of introversion in performers. "Musicians are characterized by a rich, colorful and imaginative inner mental life which renders them self-sufficient and detached from others, and therefore, apparently not naturally suited to the business of class management". Generally, studies show that persons majoring in music most generally show a preference for Intuition-Feeling (NF).

Studies reported by Thomas Wubbenhorst show a connection between creativity and androgyny. He says an androgynous person moves freely across sex-role behaviors when processing information, and so is far more flexible in this processing. Thus, creative singers would be more competent in both male and female domains. Kemp, using the Bem Sex-Role Inventory (BSRI), found that female musicians displayed divergence from traditional sex roles related to femininity found in groups of non-musicians, which may mean the female singer has more resources for managing to have both a family and a career.

Kemp also found that male musicians are strongly inclined toward sensitivity, a traditional feminine trait. He suggests that "Psychologically androgynous persons appear to be best endowed with the wider range of temperaments necessary for success in music".

There is still some question as to whether musicians are more introverted or extroverted. Wubbenhorst reported music educators to be in the category (E/I)NFJ, and performers to be ENFJ, even though Kemp finds they also have a strong tendency to introversion, indicating an inner strength in their thought processes. It seems that both instrumentalists and singers showed a consistent tendency toward introversion. I have the feeling that a singer would need to be introverted during study of the musical meaning, helped by strong intuition-feeling processes, but would need to switch to extroversion for the performance. The strong development of introversion in singers would account for the "dead-pan" expression we saw as a problem in the discussion of non-verbal communication.

In the musically talented, Kemp found anxiety in the form of excitability, threat sensitivity, and apprehensiveness. Creative types cope with the anxiety, and allow themselves to break with conventional ways of thinking, away from external regulation of work patterns and behavior.

In testing professional musicians against a control group, Kemp found a consistent pattern of expediency, a tendency to follow personal urges, and assertiveness, which combine to produce a refusal to be bound by external pressures. This pattern of non-conformity and personal autonomy has been identified in creative people. This does not mean they are undisciplined, but rather have well-internalized personal work habits.

Another point, let us not forget that Seashore long ago suggested that a case study of motor imagery would probably show that this is the outstanding characteristic of a musical temperament responsive to the musical situation. He speaks of motor images in the ear. Compare Alexander Truslit's ideas in the Mind/Body chapter (see B.Repp) and Tomatis' ear training. So add to the four pairs of personality characteristics, the musician's special response to rhythm and meter. This for instance is part of the worth of Dalcroze's work.

Kemp, too, believes the ability to internalize sound and develop a rich and comprehensive internal representation suggests that kinesthetic processes lie at the heart of compositional and interpretive processes in music. Remember Mind/Body. Physiological factors will determine some of the personality dimensions.

About musical temperament, Kyle Pruett, Yale psychologist and tenor, says that as young children, musicians attribute intense meaning to sound, hearing and feeling something in music they cannot articulate verbally. This will remain part of an adolescent singer's motivation. I have a personal memory which occurred at about nine or ten years of age. Five years in a country school had given me no musical study or experience. This was pre-television time and radios were scarce. When my across-the-road aunt got a new pedal organ, I was fascinated. The only music reading I knew was the letters assigned to the lines and spaces, and where middle C was on the keyboard. Out of my aunt's hymnal I picked "Onward, Christian Soldiers" and spent the entire afternoon painstakingly reading each chord, then pedaling it into sound. Marvelous!

Not only are the musically gifted strong in intuition and feeling, they may share with other gifted adolescents traits of curiosity, good memory, energy, thirst for knowledge, adaptability, sense of humor, imagination and problem-solving ability. Quite a personality! It is one that music teachers and parents need to understand and take into account.

Finally, there is another psychological characteristic which can stand in the way of a young, or older, singer's progress. That is, the singer is a perfectionist. In my years of teaching, I have found few who are not. We will take this up later in the context of performance.

The State of Iowa has an annual All-State Music Festival, which provides a thrilling experience to hundreds of the best High School musicians. Adolescents from all over the state vye for positions in the All-State chorus, the band, the orchestra. The ones who "make" All-State are the cream of some five or six thousand who try out. When the All-State concert is given, after a minimum time of rehearsal together, it has outdrawn the audience of a Big 12 football game. The very experienced guest conductors of these groups are always astonished and excited at the high level of performance they find, and at the serious as well as fun-loving attitude of the teen-age musicians. This is one example of the school music environment nurturing the dedicated musician. Our society needs a great deal of this.

We will go on to look at gender factors in singers' psyches

and environment. After that, we can try to see how this musical personality, with the musical brain, its marvelous mind/body functioning, its childhood musical experiences, goes to work to make a performance. Then it will be possible to see what psychological elements in talent, training, temperament and environment should be present to make a successful career.

—I am Rose, and who are you?
—Gertrude Stein/Ned Rorem

—To sing is to be.
—Rainer Maria Rilke

—And so each venture is a new beginning, a raid on the inarticulate.
—T.S.Eliot, East Coker,
Four Quartets

—Do your best, and enjoy what you are doing.
—Esther Salaman,
Unlocking the Voice

—Don't worry, be happy.
—Bobby McFerrin

CHAPTER V

Homme aux paroles pleines,

Femme aux yeux partagé

(Eluard/Poulenc)

GENDER FACTORS

As I began to consider further how singers learn, how they gain confidence in their art, and how they finally perform, I wondered what effect a difference in gender would have on all that. My first recollection was an old question: "Should women voice teachers work only with women, and men only with men?" This question has become moot in most cases, due to our gains in understanding what William Vennard called "the mechanism of voice". What we still have are social gender stereotypes which may or may not stand in the way of optimum work between student and teacher of opposite genders.

But there are other questions:

Are male and female self-concepts and confidence gained in the same way? Why does a singer believe or not believe in him or her self? How does this affect performance?

Do men and women learn differently? Does brain structure make a difference?

Does singing mean the same to a woman or a man? Can the singing actor portray both the stereotype and the non-stereotype behavior of his/her song character?

Will the male or female singer be able to gain the same patience for the long development of the voice?

Beyond the technical work, why do some female singers have difficulty developing the low register? And why do some males find it hard to get into head voice?

Why are divas more often called "difficult" than are divos?

Let us look beyond Poulenc's gorgeous song (our Chapter title) from his cycle *La Fraicheur et le Feu* (The Freshness and the Fire) to see if we can clarify some of these questions.

Since a confident self-concept is such a fundamental need for any performing artist, the effect of gender is a root question. Studies show that gender is a more powerful aspect than race or age as a child builds its picture of self. Sex is biological, being male or female. Gender, on the other hand, is socially defined masculinity and femininity, with a base in biology. It is socially defined, but the traits that are displayed are the result of a situation, its opportunities and its constraints. Due to a varying status, or social role, or amount of power the trait displayed can change rapidly.

GENDER STEREOTYPES

Beall and Sternberg summarize the gender stereotypes as follows:

Men: dominant, rational, objective, independent, decisive, competitive, aggressive, capable of leadership, good at science and math; interested in business, sports, politics.

Women: submissive, deferent toward men, emotional, subjective, gullible, dependent, sensitive to others, caring, nurturant, good at domestic tasks and child-rearing. This picture is changing, but elements hang on.

The fact is that most of these traits are inherently human, not masculine or feminine. Studies show that the strongest difference between genders lies in the area of aggressive behavior. Boys generally are more aggressive than girls. Girls show more nurturance and affiliation in their behavior. Of course there will be many individual exceptions. If you are a timid contralto you may have trouble portraying Azucena. Yet such a role might be just what you need to break through inhibition, because it is a "pretend" aggressive sound and fury. On the other hand, was Mozart making fun of the stereotype when he has Zerlina beg Masetto to beat her?

The actual difference between male and female personalities is quite small, and the difference between those within a gender can be large. Nevertheless, since gender is the earliest and most central organizing component of self-concept some of the social pattern persists. Studies find that in early adolescence, girls focus much more on expressive values, while boys emphasize instrumental values, form versus feeling. Earlier, little boys are taught to be problem-solving, and little girls are encouraged to be sensitive to others and act in a dependent way. We wish to please and to be accepted, so a boy tries to be a man and a girl tries to be a woman, socially defined.

So if society expects a certain behavior, the child will at times try to meet this expectation. Beliefs affect behavior, then behavior causes beliefs. For the budding singer, then, the girl may resist using a "commanding" voice. She under-works. the boy may resist a "soft or pleading" voice. He over-works.

CHANGING VOICES

Unless the singer sees that this behavior is not true to the real self, some trouble with vocal registers and the transition between them lies in the future—or the present. The chief passaggio lies in the same middle C octave for both genders. A woman may avoid using her chest register for fear of sounding too masculine. An anomaly to this problem is the girl who sang alto in her high school choir because she could read music well, and now she is afraid of the high notes.

Likewise, the boy, who is happy to have lost the ease of his childish falsetto when his voice changes to a man's may have trouble passing over the bridge to his head voice. An anomaly to this is the boy who loves that high freedom and finds his high baritone works as a counter-tenor. It does seem as though the high voice used in some pop styles has broken through some of this inhibition, though the pop singer may not have the classic singer's ability to bridge to the lower register.

How to handle this register difficulty brought on by gender experiences? For both male and female teachers with both boys and girls, giving a mixture of a sense of freedom and of a scientific understanding of the vocal registers and their expressiveness can bring the singer to accept the "lost" register as part of his/her true voice/self. So this is indeed as much a psychological hazard as it is a technical problem. The mixture of amount of freeing work and explanatory scientific knowledge varies with the individual, with the boys quite intrigued with the physics and physiology of their sound-making. But in forty years of teaching I have never had a girl who wasn't amazed and pleased with the grasp of how her voice works in this respect.

In Chapter I, I recommended that the teacher's piano should be placed so the student cannot see the keyboard. Then only those with absolute pitch will know how high they are singing. For the others, establishing an easy middle voice will allow them to venture unknowingly into the high area. They won't believe they sang a high A or a high C with such ease without trying to "make" it.

SELF-FULFILLING PROPHECY

There is a mechanism of self-fulfilling prophecy that can be at work between singer and teacher, coach, accompanist, colleagues, conductor, stage director, etc. To describe it simply: one person has a false idea that another will behave in a certain way, according to the stereotype, and therefore treats the other as though he will act this way. This treatment may cause the other person to so behave, trying to meet what he feels is an expectation in the first person, though this may be not at all the way he would like to behave. Actually neither person in this situation is aware of the real reason for their actions and reactions.

An example of this might occur when a female singer brings to a male teacher or coach a difficult piece of music she is very enthusiastic about learning, and she has the confidence that she can do it justice. Let's suppose this is true in this case. The coach, however, may unconsciously feel that this is too difficult for the girl. His subtle unconscious expectations of failure on her part can undermine her confident feeling, and soon, sure enough, she is not able to fully command the piece. He feels justified in leading her to a less difficult song. She feels defeated but thinks she was wrong and he was right.

In general, both women and men feel a woman's success is a matter of luck, and both feel a man's success is a matter of ability. This judgment has an effect on the person's future failure or success: a man is surer he can "do it", but a woman feels she can "do it, if she's lucky". So, again in general, men have been more sure of being successful than are women. Fortunately, this is changing to some extent, and is certainly not true in many individual cases.

It is possible this is the mechanism at work that results in a diva becoming "difficult". When having to work in a male-dominated production, she may feel the general expectation is that she will follow directions—on tempi, phrasing, timbre, ornamentation, nuances in both voice and body stage work. Fine if she agrees with all this. Both she and the production staff will be happy and "in sync". Even finer if conductor and stage director find she has insight in her work. But what if some of the expected work does not agree with her own possibly valid concept? She protests, she argues, she does not follow directions. She becomes difficult, if the director cannot at all see it her way. Maria Callas was a prime example of a female singer with valid concepts who was strong enough to enlighten her colleagues as they did her.

This brings us to see who has the power to have their way in any given situation. Generally power comes to a person having a higher status in dealing with another person. High status in life requires characteristics such as dominance, intelligence, rationality, objectivity, leadership. Each life role has its opportunities and requirements, and soon the chosen role begins to shape the personality. Western society looks at these status characteristics as essentially masculine, according to the stereotype.

On the basis of having greater knowledge, a teacher will have status in relation to a student. This is especially so in the case of one-on-one work such as teaching voice. This means the teacher has a great opportunity for influencing the student's growth, providing the teacher does not separate himself too far, due to his status, from the concerns and needs of the student.

Learning to sing well is a long process. If the singer does not feel the teacher is in sympathy with his work, he will lose motivation. The teacher must give the student opportunity to feel he is gaining power or has some control over his own development, however slowly.

This feeling of power and autonomy (not being totally dependent on the teacher) motivates the student. This undistracted concentration on integrating all his or her vocal work will help him or her gain control faster. So let the student have as much control as possible, based on knowledge.

GENDER AND CONFIDENCE

We can now see some of the ways in which self-confidence is won or lost. From the stereotypical point of view, men have an advantage in this over women. In early development a male child must find a way to change his identification with the mother in order to identify with the father. The female child, on the other hand, must pull away also from total dependence on the mother, but she will retain some part of that early identification. Therefore the boy becomes more independent, resulting in more autonomy, more confidence in his own powers, but also more separated from others. The girl, by retaining some affiliation with the mother, feels less independent, more attached to others, and so less sure of herself.

If the strongest gender difference is that boys are more aggressive, and girls more nurturant of others, this means that girls have a harder time of putting themselves forward, which is precisely what a performer has to do. Because so much of this self-feeling and the self-fulfilling prophecies are unconscious, the girl is hard put to know what to do to become the one who "shows off". Perhaps she can temporarily call up the very little girl she once was, who did show off.

Self-confidence also depends on former successes or failures. Since the woman places her chance of success on how lucky she may be in this performance, she is almost sure to expect some bad luck, and what is expected often happens. Since the man is depending on his ability which he often over-rates, his thoughts are not negative and he should have a good performance.

Women have one advantage over men, during the early part of their singing life. That is the comparative rate of maturation. Learning to sing well is a long process that tries the patience of both singer and teacher. The young male singer needs even more patience since his vocal folds are some 30% larger than the female's and his changed voice is only a few years old when he begins study. Soprano voices may be nearly mature by age 21 and may be able to perform highly demanding music. The young tenor or bass will need quite a number more years before he reaches the same technical level. It is clear he needs to understand his situation and needs a supportive teacher who helps him in every way to use his present voice well, including careful choice of repertoire. But also, the teacher should be careful not to choose songs too heavy for the apparently mature young soprano or mezzo.

In the chapter on performance we will suggest ways in which a singer can build more self-confidence.

GENDER, EMOTION, and SINGING

Part of the trust between singer and teacher will come from understanding each other's vocabulary. There is enough difference in the way men and women talk to result in misunderstanding. Developmental patterns show why. Basically men are more separate from others, women are more attached . So when men speak they tend to be forceful, sometimes loud and demanding. They speak at length in monotones, avoid eye contact, lean back and squint when listening to another. They are less likely to use terms of endearment, and are more likely to shout when frustrated. They are less inclined to confront others and bring up problems. They are short on compliments and feel uncomfortable hearing praise about themselves.

Women, on the other hand, are more complimentary and apologetic, less sarcastic and argumentative, more prone to holding grudges, answering questions with questions, and using qualifiers in their speech. They react more personally to verbal rejection. They laugh more. They look a person in the eye and lean forward when listening. They fidget less, invade other people's space less. They are gentler in touch and softer and more emotional in vocal timbre.

Men talk about things. Women talk mostly about people. Women communicate, men take action. Men and women are specialists—in their difference lies the roots of their cooperation.

Men find it difficult to describe their feelings, which may be one of the deepest reasons the singing man loves to sing. He can allow the composer and the poet to speak (sing) for him and allow his expressive singing to relieve some inhibitions. This is also true for a woman, but it is an easier revelation for her to make.

The effort to hear truly each other's language is worthwhile, because understanding is what we all need. This has been described as the "go away a little closer" message. Teachers can remember, if words fail, that men thrive on non-verbal activities.

While on the subject of emotions, we must note that the teacher may occasionally have a student suffering from depression. I have had two, both women. They were in some ways more challenging to teach because I could tell they were struggling with something, and yet they were quite rewarding because their devotion to their singing was still so strong.

One of these women was a thirty-ish faculty wife, who had two small children and a legally blind husband who needed her help with his papers. Of course she was under stress, trying to finish her own degree at the same time. To complicate my job, I had to get her to tame a Tennessee twang. The first year we worked steadily, but I thought we had reached a point where she would not want to work further. To my surprise she walked into the studio the next fall. I said "Oh! I thought you might not be back". "Well", she said "voice lessons are cheaper than the mental health clinic". That shows how deeply the results of one-on-one steady work can go.

Of course, voice teachers are not psychotherapists and should be very careful not to try to be. But it was clear to me both these students had an especially strong need to sing and a need to come for a weekly working together. Unfortunately, the rate of depression in the population is twice as high for women as for men. Women's higher risk for depression or anxiety due to long term stress is a paradox, in the context of their greater expressivity and social embeddedness.

It seems there is a connection between depression and women smoking. Some take up smoking to get some relief from depression, though this will adversely affect the voice. These students need special support, special kindness, special attention, even if they sometimes growl at you. Steadiness is all.

Hormonal and stress differences can affect the athlete-singer. Two variations in hormones make basses rather than tenors—basses have more testosterone and less estradiol.

Women are more hormonally complicated. Any imbalance

affects their mood. An altered balance of estradiol and progesterone is probably behind women's proneness to depression, and also at the root of lack of aggression. Progesterone (given externally) induces calmness. Estradiol seems to promote a sense of well-being.

Whose jaw muscles are more likely to clench? When people are tense, they tighten muscles in specific regions of the body. Women are more likely than men to clench their jaws. But a man's voice folds are more likely to tighten, so we see stress is especially interfering for all singers.

In the chapter on the musical brain we saw the gender difference in the use of the two brain hemispheres. This leads to some differences in ways of thinking and ways of learning, due to the women's verbal bias and the men's spatial bias. The socially learned gender schemas affect how memory is encoded. For women some attributes in the schema are understanding, caring, responsibility. All these require another person for expression, so women have a better memory for information encoded with reference to others. They may memorize the surrounding context, to represent the focal object or person. Women are more expert than men at reading auditory and body action cues from another, one of their ways of knowing.

Men encode memory differently due to their gender schema of independence, assertiveness, competitiveness. These require separation of self from others, therefore men have a better memory for information encoded with respect to self. So communication styles differ. Once more in general, a woman's goal is cooperation and support. A man's style is one-up-manship, competitive.

This does not mean that these schemas are what will be expressed when the memorized song poetry is performed, but only that the two genders have different ways of thinking about the material in order to encode it.

Julia Koza in her article *Big Boys Don't Cry* looks at gender as relational categories of feminine and masculine at a particular historic juncture. Her question is why more young boys don't sing in the various age-level school choirs. "Where are the males" when there are more than twice as many girls who sing? Her answer is that since men are characterized as rational and women as emotional, then sensitivity is a threat to masculinity. Therefore music, which involves emotions, seems feminine to the boy.

If singing is "sissy" (to young boys) then music teachers will try to find ways to make singing appear masculine. Boys may have the perception that high voices are unmasculine, so they prefer a low changed voice, farthest from the female range. It seems that girls are willing to sing boys' preferences for repertoire, even though the boys are not willing to reciprocate. But Koza points out it is not good for boys to avoid tender, sensitive music, so there is definitely a psychological problem here.

In sum, gender is a continuing and changing element in a singer's life. Women need to discover in themselves the assertiveness necessary to making a career. Men can find the sensitivity that changes a technically accurate performance into an artistic revelation.

> —Unis la fraicheur et le feu, Unis tes levres et tes yeux
>
> —Eluard/Poulenc

> (Unite the freshness and the fire,
> Unite your lips and your eyes)

CHAPTER VI

Vissi d'Arte, Vissi d'Amore

(Puccini/Tosca)

THE PSYCHOLOGY OF PERFORMANCE

We come now to the goal of all the previously described en-
deavors that our singer's psyche is guiding: to sing a song to
someone with all our mind/body, with all our "heart". And we come
once more to the question of why we do this, and what it means.

The bottom line of human existence is that we are part of
nature, great nature. However urban we become we do not want
to lose our connection with creation. So Samuel Barber makes a
song with daisies, another about a monk and his cat. One of my
older students said in his first year of study: "I'm beginning to
feel at one with nature". Long ago philosophers spoke of "the
music of the spheres", the movement of stars in space/time. They
didn't know this, but yes, we are made of star-dust. So something
within us remembers this part of who we are.

We also have memories of all our own experiences and behaviors since infancy. It is not enough to only speak of all this
"who we are", because some of it cannot be said in words, and
all of it can only be expressed as fully as possible in words plus
music, that is, song. To communicate all this, to celebrate, to
question, the voice must be raised, vowels expanded, rhythms
felt, tones given a special timbre. We must communicate. We
must perform. This is our "heart".

Poets and song composers express some of this "heart" in characters whom the singer must portray. The character shown or implied gives the first layer of the performance, as in *Die Winterreise*, in which the young man makes a winter journey, crying for his lost love. What the singer/actor must remember is that these characters are not real people. They are imaginative creations in the poet's or librettist's mind. The descriptions of the character and the situation give useful information for the singer's presentation. But if you look carefully you see that the character does not act or think just like a real person. To be faithful to the vision of the poet and composer, the singer must understand that there are deeper patterns of relationship and development. Why, for instance, is the journey taken in winter? There is an obvious answer, but the singer needs to continue imagining, continue feeling, continue thinking, to portray the desolation of the poems and the sense of a mind's journey.

It will take time, caring, imagination, intuition, visualization to bring up what is so important about often mundane elements in the text, and about this special musical structure. Teachers can teach, coaches coach, peers can suggest, and all this is helpful, but no one can tell the singer what to find and feel with his special mind/body, his musical brain, his persona. He must discipline and stretch his psyche to do the work, ever growing, ever improving, never perfect. He must be in love with, devoted to, the work, whatever it may be.

FIVE PARTS

There are five parts in performance preparation, all of which are basic to comfortable and excitingly expressive presentation. First is the study of the musical/poetic work, over a considerable period of time, so that it becomes thoroughly known. We store in our musical brain all the meanings we can imagine, and a concept of all the feelings that give nuance to the meaning. Then, in performance, we do not do things to the music—we let the music do things to us. Psychologically, we must love the song, love the singing, and above all, be patient.

Second, we must learn how to deal psychologically with all the conditions of performance. This too must be thought about and learned over a long period of time. The chief condition different from practice is facing an audience, with the feeling you have something to give that is worth their while and worth all your work.

Third, is a working through of growth change in the first two parts, that continually builds one's feeling of self-knowledge, self-worth, self-confidence.

The fourth part is what is usually thought of first, the technical proficiency of the instrument. All through the training years and the earlier years of adult singing, the ease and quality of the sound produced and the freedom of body/mind production should improve. This leads to ever more trust in the vocal instrument, so that we learn to accept the few times it fails to be at its best, and we learn how to get right back on track.

Finally, the performance situation has mechanics (tuned piano, hall acoustics, program notes, recording equipment, stage lighting, etc.) of which we must be clearly aware and in command.

These five parts are mixed all through the performance, so that over the whole study/training time they must all be worked at simultaneously. The results will be a happy performer, not too nervous to sing in public, and who truly experiences the wonderful joy of singing. Angelika Kirschlager describes her teacher (Opera News, August 1999) Gerhard Kahry at the Vienna Academy. "He is a very Italian tenor, who sings with his whole body. He sees a singer as a whole, everything belongs together—mentality, character, and problems—everything makes a singer".

PERFECTIONISM

I asked soprano Ericka Wueschner how her work had gone with a teacher in Juilliard in New York City, whose teaching I respect. "Wonderfully", she said, "she absolutely makes you understand what you are doing".

It is this necessary understanding that can cause problems for the perfectionist singer. With all the expectations accumulated from parents, teachers, coaches, intendants, directors, conductors, peers, and one's own ego ideal, it may become very difficult to feel one's performance is adequate.

I see this need to be perfect in student after student, lesson after lesson. They sing a vocalise or a song phrase and I see the look of dissatisfaction creep over their faces. They are telling themselves it was not good enough, and it should be better. The next time they try it, they are going to work harder to make it right—just exactly what they should not do.

Singers all work too hard—getting set to begin the sound, then trying to get everything just right, every pitch, every vowel and syllable, every rhythm. This chopped-up mental and physical labor just gets in the way of the bright, free, and accurate sound we want. Most of this work should be done before singing, before memorizing, so that the mental picture of our work is clear and the instrument can do its work. As Benita Valente says (tapping her head): "This is what we are training".

The singer's aim, of course, is to make the finest performance possible at the moment. So many things can go wrong. It is a wise singer who realizes that the goal of perfection will always be aimed for but will move away and never be reached, that the process of aiming toward that goal is what is important, that making mistakes is allowed, that furthermore there is no one perfect in the audience, not even one's teacher.

The fact that singers make recordings raises the bar of perfect performance, as the following story shows. It seems a soloist and a conductor finally agreed on the version of a recording they would release. "It sounds pretty good, doesn't it?" says the soloist. "Yes", says the conductor, "don't you wish you could sing that well?" Students can mistakenly compare their singing to that on records.

During practice, the singer may have trouble with a pitch or a word in a phrase. If this small part is attempted over and over again, it will continue in performance to be a stopping point, not part of the ongoing song. Singers tend to try too hard to "fix" difficult parts. They will be better off if they clarify the problem mentally but try less hard and allow the difficulty to disappear in the corrected flow of sound. Many times restoring the vowel resonance line accomplishes this.

Allowing the production to be free will ease the distress of not being perfect. If perfection is pursued, the singer may continue to think that because he makes errors he is not a worthy person, and that worsens the anxiety. The concept of *allowing* the sound to happen leads to a more spontaneous production.

There is a double trap for the perfectionist. On the one hand there is the realistic need to do very well. On the other hand, there is a fear of the consequences of not doing well. The need and the fear are both stressful. The singer must have high standards—this is not the problem. The problem comes when perfectionism causes so much emotional stress that one cannot succeed or cannot feel happy at work. One feels tension, frustration, even anger, and a fear of humiliation for one's shortcomings. The conflict is between *knowing* one is good enough but *feeling* "I am just not good enough".

One perfectionist symptom in a singer is not being able to accept praise. A teacher may feel a student is making excellent progress and wants to encourage his self-confidence. The perfectionist student cannot tolerate hearing praise when he is so certain he is falling short, and certain the falling short is more important than the actual accomplishment.

It is true that it is difficult for a perfectionist to change his beliefs, such as:

—If I do it perfectly, I will be satisfied.
—If I do it perfectly, everyone will praise me.
—If I make a mistake, I am humiliated.

—I will be rejected if I'm not perfect.

—If I'm not perfect, then I'm a worthless singer.

The singer needs to realize that with these beliefs there is no way he can be liberated from the fear of making a mistake, nor can he ever be perfect enough to feel he deserves approval or praise. He must realize he has lost his satisfaction, not to speak of joy, in singing well. He must ask himself how he needs to think differently and then do differently. "What can I change?" He needs to learn what is possible for him, and what is acceptable. He needs to justify his own wobbly positive thoughts by drawing all the acceptance and sincere good judgments he can, from his teachers, peers, and friends.

It can be helpful to aim for a "good" performance, rather than trying for the "best". One's "best" can happen only once in a lifetime, so that aiming for it every time brings failure. Failure brings feelings that one is not worthy, that perhaps one will be rejected when judged to be imperfect. If "best" can be attained just once, then "good" is a reasonable goal every time. My teacher, Paola Novikova, on the necessity of an established technique upon which the singer's psyche can depend: "We sing gorgeously perhaps four times a year, but there is never any excuse for not singing well".

PERFORMANCE ANXIETY

Of all the psychological facets of singing, by far the most study has been made of performance anxiety, "stage fright". I will summarize here what is currently known about the causes for and coping with this anxiety. Excellent technique does not always free one from excessive nervousness. Luciano Pavarotti (Opera News, September 1982): "The audience has no idea how terrified singers are. I have spent twenty years walking out on that stage, wondering what is going to happen. The longer you sing, the more responsibility you have". Even Caruso was intensely nervous before performance. He felt unable to sing until he reached his dressing room and donned his costume. He felt he had to struggle desperately hard to reach the top of his profession, and once there had to hold on with all his strength.

At one seminar on performance anxiety I was chatting about it with another voice teacher whom I shall not name. She told me her defeating experience and wrote it out longhand for me: "Stage fright has been the most debilitating experience in my singing career. I found it necessary to just stop performing because of it, even to the point where I would not vocalise. It loomed enormously in every dimension of my performance: dryness of voice, almost as if bile was coming up in my throat. This made me self-conscious, with extreme heart palpitation, a fear of loss of memory, of losing my balance on stage, a fear of fellow performers losing their thought and causing me to lose my place. I have literally skipped nine pages of Menotti's *The Telephone* on stage, throwing the baritone completely off. This was a complete failure. Not only did I lose voice, with cracking, but I would begin to laugh uncontrollably. This is my story of this terrible dragon".

This sad story is at one end of the tension/arousal spectrum. At the other end is a rare singer like Mary Garden who claimed she never felt nervous. In the middle is someone like Benita Valente who tells how nervous she was at her Metropolitan Opera audition. She says she was shaking, thinking she could not sing . . . then as she walked on stage she told herself to try and do what she did as a child, to forget all the lessons, forget all the words, and sing purely and simply as she did as a child. It worked.

There are various reasons for experiencing performance anxiety. The most obvious one is simply not being fully prepared, or not having a dependable singing technique. There are other reasons for not having the self-confidence to cope with the excess fright that brings on the symptoms of rapid heart beat, dry mouth, shaking hands or knees, short breath, sweaty palms, etc. Inner body symptoms are a rise in blood pressure and muscle tension. A deeper psychological effect is a sense of impending doom. Paola Novikova, with all her complete preparation and artistic abilities, told me she suffered stage fright so that "I would stand in the wings and wish the roof or the walls would fall in. I would have to be pushed on stage. Then I was all right".

Sometimes a colleague can help a performer. Robert Merrill would walk Jussi Bjoerling around the block, telling him how great he was, that he had nothing to fear. Notes on Angel recording S-3697 has Dietrich Fischer-Dieskau speaking on the great accompanist Gerald Moore's retirement: "We artists, turning grey from constant stage fright, know that this 'youngster' with a great past, has always shone like a lighthouse in the seas of our anxieties".

One of the strongest causes of stage fright is perfectionism, the setting of unrealistically high standards. Dr. Garland Y. DeNelsky at the 1985 Aspen Symposium on Performance Anxiety gave me permission to use his model for development of the anxiety:

(1) much early reinforcement for performance
(2) performance becomes the basis of self-esteem
(3) increasing competition among performers
(4) highly critical judges, negative feedback
(5) perfection becomes the goal of performance
(6) highly practiced behavior becomes de-automatized and unreliable
(7) individual obsesses more and more about a negative outcome
(8) (unconsciously) performance anxiety mounts
(9) a "positive feedback loop" is created, so that making a mistake equates with failing as a human being.

According to Alan Keaton, the mastery of the autonomic nervous system is the core of our discussion. This system is divided into the *sympathetic*, which prepares for the fight or flight symptoms, and the *parasympathetic*, which stimulates digestive function. He says this system, the chief mechanism by which emotion or anxiety is expressed, can be tuned to appropriate levels through heart rate control. Heart rates increase or decrease depending on our emotional state.

The individual who is well-conditioned and/or emotionally tuned has a slower heart rate, and we can learn to control both fear and exertion in order to lower the rate. Keaton suggests that a singer test his heart rate 40 minutes before a performance, by putting a finger on wrist or neck pulse and counting that for 15 seconds. Multiply by four and you have your rate. If it is over 80, some calming action is needed.

The panic can be lowered by sitting quietly, breathing slowly and deeply, and visualizing a tranquil scene. After this, do an easy walking back and forth, breathing in for 4 steps, holding breath for 4 steps, then exhaling for 4 steps, and repeat. This should reduce anxiety and get the body into an easy moving feeling before going on stage. Supplement C has more body control, heart rate reducing, resources. It is important to know that studies have shown that the use of tranquilizers does not help the anxious singer.

Keaton has two further suggestions for anxiety tuning. In the stress of preparing for and reaching a performance, a singer may forget his necessary habit of drinking 8 glasses of water a day, to the detriment of his autonomic system. Further, if a singer/actor has discovered that he or she will have a greater performance ability if the use of a certain vitamin or specific activity is repeated four times a day, just the process of reminding himself—this is great and it really works—has a positive effect. It boosts the autonomic nervous system, and chemical changes can be measured which account for this sense of well-being.

Eloise Ristad's book *A Soprano On Her Head* is a great help in de-fusing those awful outside and inside-our-head judges, who cannot be satisfied. Tell them to stop criticizing and to support you in your goals, in your progress.

On the psychological front, two general attitudes must be gained. The first is to appreciate the *process* of working on a goal, instead of being impatient to reach and over-valuing the goal itself. The lifelong process of growth will help us attain goals beyond our present vision. The second is to achieve a realistic self-esteem in place of a feeling of failure or self-doubt.

There are some ten common cognitive distortions in performing situations:

> *All or nothing thinking*—if not perfect, it is a failure.
> Overgeneralization—continuous failure from one negative.
> *Mental filter*—one negative detail makes whole situation negative.
> *Disqualifying the positive*—to keep a negative belief.
> *Jumping to conclusions*—thinking the worst without sorting facts.
> *Magnifying imperfections and minimizing good points.*
> *Emotional reasons*—being overwhelmed by music which distorts reason.
> *"Should" statements*—fostering guilt feelings by "I should do this". Think "should statements" positively, such as "I should practice this slowly and accurately".
> *Labeling and mislabeling*—the student labels himself a failure rather than describing and then correcting his error.

To counteract these distortions, the performer must discard negative thoughts, putting himself down, all that has been humorously described as "awfulizing", and must tell himself positive messages. "This is possible for you". "You are improving; be happy". "My goal is to share this music, not to be perfect". "I am a winner because I do my best". The ones who do not do their own best are losers.

The singer who has incorporated unrealistic expectations can establish realistic ones. Growth means change, which can feel threatening, so the singer must be brave to accept growth in himself and in his vocal powers. He can be happy with small improvements, because such gradual almost unnoticeable improvements are what lead in the long run to solid accomplishment. The fear of failure is difficult to fight, but the singer must try to realize how unrealistic it is to be totally perfect. I point out to students that baseball players are paid enormous salaries if they can hit the ball slightly more than once in four tries. That means they "fail" 75% of the time. Failure is expected, and the singer can allow himself to expect it too, although singers' averages are much higher for less pay! Accept the possibility, even choose a passage in which to fail. It is allowed. We are not gods, we are human. It is that vulnerable humanity we are communicating in songs.

While I was adding ceramics to my teaching, I became acquainted with the world's great potters and pottery, so I told my students about the best Japanese potters who deliberately leave a mistake in their pots, "because only God is perfect". Similarly, Arabian weavers leave a wrong thread in their magnificent weavings.

What the singer needs to realize is how much these negative thoughts and fears freeze him and tense him up. In this state he cannot make use of his innate abilities nor learn well, that is, accept new developments in his voice as they happen. Singers worry whether they are on pitch, whether the sound is good, whether the voice will break, whether they have enough breath for the phrase, etc. While they are hunting for all these things that can go wrong, they are interfering with the confidence that allows the sound to flow.

Gaining this ease, with a not-to-worry attitude, eventually brings enough breath, warm sound, correct pitch. At first my students may think this letting go, this not-worrying implies low performance standards; but finally they understand what "letting go" of tensions, "letting-go" of fears can do for them. They can keep their minds on their music, not on themselves.

Two other practices will help release the performer from the perfectionist rules. First, in practice, anchor one's body/mind rhythms into the rhythms of the song by dancing it, first without singing, and then as one sings. Feeling that rhythm, so related to body rhythms of heart and breath, will enhance the flow of the sound. This flow takes away the rough hesitations to see if the pitch is right, etc. The dancing also releases the voice, and some of this release will remain in performance so the voice can be trusted to work.

Another practice is to improvise. Singers must spend much time and energy memorizing someone else's creations. They need to take time to realize and practice the fact that they are musicians, and that music truly comes from the inside out. There is much they can discover by making small spontaneous songs, cries, vocalises of their own, as a way of channeling energy, of expressing feelings, of letting beautiful or interesting sounds be free and just surprisingly happen. One year I had much fun on our faculty recital, doing a five-minute improvisation called "Bird Songs, Whale Songs, and Scrawny Cries". The scrawny cries thought came from a Wallace Stevens poem which made me think of the first cries of spring and awakening in this universe. So I improvised responses to and elaborations of taped bird and whale songs with my own "cries". Not perfection, but satisfying, and fully interesting to the audience. A friend in the audience who is a farmer, a bee-keeper, and an ex-high school counselor, told me he was almost moved to tears.

Wesley Balk's books have excellent suggestions for improvisations that free one from the "rules". Doing the gibberish he describes is hilarious and strengthens one's feelings of rhythm and of speaking clear consonants. While improvising one can do no wrong, never fail.

A number of therapists working on anxiety of all kinds have found visualization to be a help. It is best to begin by relaxing, either sitting comfortably or lying on the floor. Take plenty of time and feel the easy deep breathing. Then begin visualizing a walk through a place that is beautiful, peaceful, comforting. See and hear everything you can in this place. Mary Ann Hanley in her article on creative visualization recommends meeting "a counselor" in this sanctuary, a "friend who will give you guidance, support and inspiration".

Then begin visualizing the place where you will perform, pretending it is right next to your sanctuary. Go through the whole performance in your mind, seeing yourself coming on stage feeling ready to communicate, singing, and succeeding.

This kind of visualizing helps to establish more positive thoughts about one's performance. Oddly enough, it also helps to think ahead of time about all the things that can possibly go wrong, "awful-izing", and decide what to do in each case. This is phobia de-sensatization technique, in which the anxious singer imagines all his fears and sets them up in a schedule of least to most fearful. Then, while relaxing, he begins with the least fearful possibility and keeps imagining it until the anxiety goes away. He de-sensitizes himself as far up the list as he can toward the greatest fear. Not only does this technique diminish an unreasonable amount of fear, it can also change the singer's idea of how he can handle it.

For the learning or early professional singer, the more often you perform or audition, the more excess anxiety disappears. You look forward to the performance as an opportunity to communicate, and to the audience as friends. In your preparation, leave room for spontaneity. Performance is exploring, learning, growing, sharing, not being perfect.

PERFORMANCE

We have so far pulled out many facets of the singer's psychology from the general motivations, processes and circumstances of singing. To see what is involved in performance, we need to integrate these facets into an insightful pattern. We have to think of technical production, stage presence and move-

ment, concepts of musical and poetic meaning, character portrayal, and all-over passionate involvement, as having parallel
or conflicting psychological bases which all come together to
make up the whole performance.

In every performance, whether of songs or a stage work, there
is a character who sings, characters who are sung to, and internal and external circumstances of these characters that lead to
the sung message. The persons sung to can be other characters,
or the audience, or sometimes oneself. We have already noted
that the singer conveys this message through nuances of vocal
tone, text dynamics and emphases, rhythm, stage movement, and
non-verbal communication by face and body. All of this grows
out of the concept of the character singing and those sung to.

This specific characterization is possible for the singer/actor
because of the way the persona is built. We, each of us, assume
or play out a variety of roles, in order to function in our everyday
environment, in our career, and in any special set of circumstances we encounter, such as travel, bad luck, competition, etc. As
we noted earlier, adding all the current roles together make up our
personality, and that will constitute a great part of our sense of self.

I understand the dynamics of role-playing better when I recall the roles I assumed as a twenty-year-old college graduate
going to New York to study voice, art, dance. The chief roles to
work at or just accept were: the daring role of the would-be singer/
artist, the economic role of the poor student in the Depression,
the competent role of a recreational group leader (music, art,
drama, folkdance). When we play roles we are adapting to an
environment and creating a form for our thoughts and feelings.
The question is, will we play the role of victim or survivor? We try
to master a bit of reality within an appropriate context when the
external circumstances coincide with inner readiness. These different functions of the self are what make it possible for us to
imagine we are a particular character in a song or stage work.
Robert Landy has a most helpful description of how all this works.

Jonathon Dunsby and Shirlee Emmons have thorough descriptions of ways of establishing these characters.

What must happen in an artistic performance is that for the duration of the work the singer becomes the character without losing himself. This means he is not simply an actor *showing* the audience how this character might feel and act. This is superficial, and the audience cannot be deeply moved, nor the singer truly satisfied. The singer, even for a three-minute song, must construct a life story and a lifestyle for his character—how did this character come to this point of expression? This gives the singer a rich number of possibilities for doing what we call "interpretation" of the music and the poem.

The singer/actor faces a difficulty in becoming such a fully realized character. This character has a personality he must for the time being assume. He must temporarily step outside his own personality and let his "character" take over. But here is a danger. This must not go too far. He must be both "me" and "not-me", still himself and yet fully in another character. My voice teacher colleague, who wrote about her stage anxiety, got lost in her "Telephone" character and laughed uncontrollably. This loss of control happened to a famous tenor in a *Werther* performance at the Metropolitan Opera, when the grief of the character caused him to break down and cry uncontrollably. Sopranos have a problem playing dying heroines, because "crying" can become uncontrollable when one is worked up.

Remember Yeats' famous question: "How do you separate the dancer from the dance?" In every performance the artistic singer will try to reach that state, of being at the same time the fully expressive character, and the self who is directing and monitoring the performance. The singer must forget himself, forget his singing. He must not do too much, not try to be perfect, just be the character. My first nearest achievement of this dual state was in singing Mme. Flora in *The Medium*. I had never before made such an intense characterization, yet simultaneously experiencing a cool managing, directing of that characterization, and this endured throughout all the scenes. Some singers in great operas are so intense in character they need hours after the final curtain to come back to themselves, out of character. Some musical theater performers who have many performances per week simply find it easier to stay in character.

In his preparation, the performer has sorted out unimportant things, put distractions aside, then concentrated directly on the things important to his success. This settles his self-confidence, especially when he reminds himself of the strengths of his performance.

This singer has learned from former mistakes, so that he has established right rather than wrong ways of presentation. All of this puts him in control of his instrument, his self, his communicating.

How can the singer, who already has the voice and the performing elements trained, reach this state of concentration and calm in which the consistently focused performance can be made? Let us review the factors we have already studied. Efficient perceptual-motor action has four elements: good body alignment, clear mental concepts, relaxed concentration, and awareness of body feedback.

Emotional motivation furnishes the key energy base. The singer must strongly feel the need to communicate, to give, to share. Any strong pressure to sing perfectly must be reduced, so that the singer has the attitude of aiming for success, not one of fearing failure. The performer feels positive about his self, that this gift of being able to sing well is important and that his realistic self-esteem will enable him to share his loved music with an audience. He is ready to meet the challenge of performance.

The goal of readiness for performance is a thoroughly trained healthy vocal instrument with which a well trained body/mind produces a unique expressive sound. All parts need to be continually worked at together. Then the singer will achieve what is necessary on stage: automation of the vocal mechanism, automation of the musical technique, automation of the action. Only then can the singer be free to concentrate on the meanings and how to express these truly.

In the next chapter we will take up the psychological principles by which greater artistry can be achieved. For now, the following brief summary may help us grasp the complexity of having a song in the psyche.

First we have the basic instrumental 3-P's mentioned at the beginning of the book: Physiology, Physics/vowel acoustics, and Psychology. On the knowledge of these functions the vocal instrument is built. It is built by the 3-P's of mental and physical action: Practice, Persistence, and Patience. This action gives the 5-C's of psychological result: Confidence, Concentration, Consistency, Creativity, and hopefully a little Charisma.

This also works in the other direction. The singer gains in his 5-C's psychological skills. This enables him to practice, persist, and be patient with his progress. From this he gains knowledge about the 3-P's functioning of his instrument, and from all this the free voice emerges. In fact, this structure is working in both directions all through the singer's life from beginning to end.

—One cannot walk out on stage as though one were going shopping.

—Lotte Lehman
(NATS Bulletin March 1991)

—That scrawny cry... It was/A Chorister whose c preceded the choir... /It was like/A new knowledge of reality.
Not about the thing but the thing itself.

—Wallace Stevens

—I am that final thing A man learning to sing.

—Theodore Roethke

—The sound of singing so changes me, I wonder who I ever was.

—Mark Van Doren

CHAPTER VII

Io son l'umile ancella del genio creator
(Cilea, Adriana Lecouvreur)

REALIZING THE SINGER'S FULL POTENTIAL

Of the multitude of singers ready for some performance, most will sing as many years as they can as devoted amateurs. A very few will begin to take the daunting psychological step of thinking about making a career. These singers need to get information about the singing career lifestyle, and they need to question their teachers. The teachers need to question their students.

It takes a certain personality and temperament to tolerate and cope with the extremely difficult singer's life. It takes a strong body to travel, to get through long or stressful rehearsals, to perform, and go on to the next all different production. It takes someone who can bear to be away from home a great deal, and who can simplify this complicated work enough to keep time and space for family, roots, and self. It takes one who can live a fairly Spartan life in order to nurture the vocal cords and the energetic body.

To summarize this performance lifestyle: there is travel, dry planes, fatigue, loneliness, ugly and impersonal surroundings, throat anxiety, bad food, too much talk at parties, air pollution, new repertoire to learn, new conductors, new stage directors, new colleagues, new theater, stages sloped or otherwise interfering with breathing, critics; and so why would a singer want a professional career? Finding work and keeping the voice are the very first problems. There are endless auditions and competitions which require a strong psyche to survive disappointments. Why a career? Because not only does this singer have a superior voice and the mental and physical abilities to manage this lifestyle, there is nothing that gives him/her the joy that singing does. This singer feels he/she must sing, must sing greatly loved music, must sing better and better. The greatest career reward is simply the chance to sing for people, to share the music, the message, the understanding, the feelings, the ecstacy.

The audience is empathetic to a performance of soaring sound and mind/body expression that frees their bodies, minds, and imaginations. This in turn causes the singer's spirit to soar. This is the language not of science, but of psychological experience, and this is why singers must sing.

Most career singers need to stay with the good teacher they have found, in order to keep and improve their voices through all the years of good and less good performance. When I began my study with Paola Novikova the last two years of her life, Nicolai Gedda had been with her for ten years, George London for sixteen, and they both were singing gorgeously. Frank Sinatra vocalized every day, and all through the years of his career he kept working with three successive opera singers, whom he found "knew how to maintain the equipment". A good teacher will help a singer to never sing beyond his strength. "Spend the interest, not the capital" is common vocal advice, "and always study".

The decision to attempt a singing career usually is made in the undergraduate senior year, roughly age 21. Only the exceedingly exceptional singer will be ready to look for work at this point. Several more years of preparation and maturation are usual and needed, so the first next step entails putting together a graduate type of study which would include an exceptional teacher, several languages, coaching, stage play, movement training, learning roles, learning about the music business, and in general toughening up psychological resilience. The Hanine Roussel book about Giulietta Simoniato will convince anyone of the wisdom of long patient preparation of vocal technique and stage presence, and its wonderful rewards.

Since very few will have major careers, the teacher must be truthful with the student about his prospects. The singer must know and be honest with himself about his abilities, and compare where he is with the complete package he will need. The teacher's work at this level is to help the singer integrate what he already knows into a spellbinding performance.

Later, to put all this necessary preparation to work, one possible second step is to audition at an established opera company for their training program. Sanford Sylvan reported at a National Association of Teachers of Singing Convention (Philadelphia, 2000) that in his first two years in New York he sang in 103 auditions! There are some 93 competitions each year in the United States, and an additional 55 around the world. By this time the singer must show personality, individuality, stage presence, energy, musicality, physical appearance, responsibility, survival instincts, and yes, VOICE. Many singers at this point have good voices, good technique, but lack the expression which comes from knowing style and nuances of language, and from daring to take risks. Shirlee Emmons gives three basic reasons why a better performer lies dormant: either the potential is hidden by cultural or social forces, or the singer does not believe in himself, or he does not know how to use his potential. Emmons has excellent suggestions for solving this dilemma. Richard Miller in *On the Art of Singing* gives some clear guidelines for preparation for performance success.

The singer can make a different choice than a professional career, and that is the very honorable, rewarding, and even exciting decision to sing in his own community or area. The better prepared he is the more thrill he gets from the singing and the sharing—a true amateur or semi-professional lover of song. This leaves room for some other creative career and for a fuller family life. Teachers can be happy teaching these good singers, because the more there are who sing for the enjoyment, the better for our society's musical life and development.

SINGER-TEACHER RELATIONSHIP

Before we launch into the psychology involved in becoming an ever better singer, let us look at the singer-teacher relationship, both conscious and unconscious, that underlies part of the singer's training and further development. Students somehow receive psychic gifts from their teachers, but what is less recognized is that they in turn have brought the teacher very special psychic gifts. It is truly due to this giving and taking that both are able to grow.

It is not easy to put this mutual influence into words, but here are some of the teacher's gifts. Many have been implied in earlier chapters, but here we can be explicit on how the teacher's growth affects and is affected by the student.

First, the teacher keeps in mind that the singer, not the teacher, teaches himself. What the teacher gives is factual information and psychological support. I agree with Richard Miller that true factual information does not make singing more complex—"it makes it more direct and simplistic". The more enthusiastic the teacher is about the correct information he is able to give, the more likely the student will make happy use of it. The student does the work, not the teacher. "The more imaginative and scientifically based the teaching", Friedrich Brodnitz says, "the more wiggle room the student has. The impact of the voice teacher on the student comes from a combination of authoritative advice, right choice of words, and a compassionate tone".

The teacher must give this advice in small doses and never in a negative way. As Lamperti said, "never say to a student 'you sing badly'". I seldom tell a student which of his vocal problems

I am aiming at. Only when he has conquered it do I ask him to look back and realize what and how he has improved. This remembering exactly what work he has done for what purpose will stand him in good stead in keeping his voice healthy in the future. Of course the teacher's earlier guidance must have been clear and memorable.

After the gift of information, the teacher's most important gift is that he and his judgment can be trusted. Without trust nothing will work. With it, the student will feel more trustful of himself and his voice, and will want to win the teacher's trust that he is serious about his singing. This means each takes responsibility for his part of the work.

The teacher's gift of careful listening is as important as the gift of giving directions, of telling the student what to do. The work of giving directions must not use up the listening time— listening to the singing, of course, but also to what the student says both in words and in body language.

When the student needs to speak of something in his experience, or has questions, the teacher may in turn tell a self-story that appropriately echoes the student's concern. The student then knows he has been heard.

Empathic listening does not mean being kind, sympathetic, etc. It means a way of listening from inside another's experience that brings appreciation of that person's frame of reference. This warm studio atmosphere also allows the teacher to encourage the shy student to socialize, because the professional singer must be able to get along comfortably with not only family and friends but with colleagues and staffs everywhere he sings. The teacher can encourage the student's realistic positive self-talk: "I'm really OK", which builds self-confidence and skill development.

However, the teacher must be careful not to meddle with the tender psyche of a singer whose sound-making shows he is having some complex psychic problems. Teachers must remember to do no harm. In such a case, it seems wise to concentrate not on the problems but on the technique, which can free the voice which may free the psyche. The Deborah Rosen and Robert Sataloff article on *Self-Esteem and Singers* is especially helpful in drawing the line.

"A teacher's career . . . exacts of every one of us a constant balance between our reasoning faculties and our spontaneous instincts. We have to weigh the pros and the cons, to harmonize the present, the past and the future. to dispense with useless thoughts and gestures, to be both serious and lighthearted, strict and lenient, imaginative and constructive, artists and artisans, doers

and dreamers, teachers and pupils, ever bent on establishing equilibrium between the progress we should call forth in others and that which we should ourselves realize for the joy and security of future generations". This is E. Jacques-Dalcroze in *Eurhythmics, Art and Education*, page 246. It is not 21st century language, but it is true psychology.

The student will pick up on the teacher's aesthetic attitude, on his life philosophy, on his professional standards, on his attitudes about his own career and the role of music in society. So in weighing all this the student works not only on his voice but on a model for his professional self.

THE PSYCHOLOGICAL 5-C'S OF ARTISTIC GROWTH

There are two basic facts underlying and affecting the psychology of the singer. The first is the point made earlier, that the voice is totally and continually revealing of the singer's self.

The second fact is true of all performance—its transitory nature. Unlike painters, writers, and scientists, singers have no final product to show. The performance is past. It is true there are recordings and videotapes, but this is technology performing, not the singer. To have the experience, the singer must do it again. And again.

The singer can in no way change these two facts, that he

reveals and bares himself, and that his performance disappears when the air waves stop.

To project making a life's work as a singer in the face of these two basic situations takes tremendous courage. This "humble servant" must summon all his/her psychological strength to become the creative singer he/she wants to be.

It would be just as well for the teacher not to stress these facts to his student, but even when the singer is not clearly noticing them, they still will affect his motivation to sing and to sing better. This will take confidence-building, much concentration on both technique and message, becoming a consistent rather than an up-and-down performer, adding to the creativity of his total work, and reaping some charisma in being the self that accomplishes all this.

CONFIDENCE

Ryan Allen is a fine bass who travels all over the country to perform challenging roles with established regional opera companies, and who also works as a house singer at the Metropolitan Opera. In a personal communication he told me: "Confidence is a quality which will vary in individuals and wax and wane in any one individual. The voice cannot issue forth in the utmost expression of a singer's talent if he or she is not confident".

Allen says "a difficulty with one's confidence comes with letting oneself be 'psyched out'. Remarks by the conductor, stage director, colleagues or a newspaper critic can undermine a singer. A negative atmosphere erodes confidence. The mind becomes the singer's enemy as he or she dwells on what he or she perceives as a crack in the foundation. Soon the singer has manufactured a series of cracks which are not present and perceives his or her foundation crumbling. Talent is choked off, and in the extreme, the singer feels he or she can do nothing without stumbling".

Allen continues: "Auditions are also a problem in this area.

Most auditions do not lead to casting, and singers typically feel rejected. This leads to a slow degradation of confidence. The singer must reflect that his or her product is good and worthy, and repeat that over and over. An individual must throw up a wall to keep out negativity. If a singer is not strong enough to do this, he or she cannot have a career".

Let's start with the lightest part of confidence building—a sense of humor. Without this sense, the singer is apt to take everything that happens personally, and this he cannot manage well. Much of this lack goes back to perfectionism. If he makes a mistake which actually does not blow down the theater nor devastate the singing ensemble, he should be able to see the humor of his momentary imperfection and see how clever he can be to cover it, then laugh it off after the show. Equally, it helps to see the humor in production difficulties and in everyday life mishaps and challenges.

The singer's teacher certainly needs a sense of humor, so that lessons can be joyous experiences. The teacher must not be overcautious, as Victor Fields says, "with an overdose of rules and warnings". The voice functions best when the singer is buoyant and exhilarated. Carefree attitudes are conducive to vocal freedom. Laughter is an exercise that will improve freedom. Robert Edwin in his *Bach to Rock Connection* article in the NATS Journal, Sept/Oct 1990, suggests kinds of fun vocalises a teacher may introduce in a lesson to lighten the serious work.

Soprano Helen Donath, another Novikova student, agrees with this. She sent me the text of an interview with her in which she says "One only lives if one has the courage for joy and sorrow. The most beautiful thing in my profession is the contact with people. That I can reach people so that they laugh or cry, that they feel".

To have at least one moment of laughter, I usually start off a lesson with my "joke of the week", preferably a musical joke. For example, when Beverly Sills began to pursue a career, she tells how she came to sing in a suburb of Kearney, Nebraska.

There was an epidemic of cattle hoof-and-mouth disease raging at the time. When she saw a local newspaper coverage of her upcoming concert, on the front page was a picture of a dead cow with the caption, "Beverly Sills comes to sing recital". On another page was her picture, and the caption was "hoof-and-mouth disease victim". No wonder she is called "Bubbles".

Or if a student has trouble understanding his translation of a foreign language song text, I tell him this true story that happened on a trip through Talinn, Estonia, coming from St. Petersburg to Moscow. We went to buy tickets to the ballet, and asked the ticket seller what ballet was to be given that evening. She answered in good Estonian, and we had to tell her we couldn't understand. She scratched her head, looked doubtful, and finally said "I think—I think—it is Swan Pond!"

If a singer has lost confidence due to some music critic's statement, he may take heart when reminded of Bernard Shaw's definition of a critic as "a writer who leaves no turn unstoned!"

Not only will laughter free the voice, but according to Dr. Leo S. Black, laughter researcher at Loma Linda University School of Medicine in California, mirthful laughter activates cells that decrease pain and boost the immune system. That's one more defense for vocal health.

Beyond knowing we can make laughable mistakes, there is much to know about our strengths, weaknesses, and abilities. Only self-understanding can build realistic self-esteem. Only self-esteem can build confidence.

Christopher Bollas, in *Being a Character*, sets out a persuasive theory of how a person gains a feeling of self, and how this self can gain strength and spiritual growth, the basis of the singer's confidence. Very briefly put, he proposes that our unconscious mind gets filled on the one hand with repressed memories of early traumas, and on the other with ideas related to present experience that need to be temporarily protected from interference by the conscious mind. This double unconscious development is echoed by Wordsworth (whose name was his destiny) who wrote:

> These obstinate questionings
> of sense and outward things,
> Fallings from us, vanishings,
> Blank misgivings of a creature
> Moving about in worlds not realized.

The pre-verbal "repressed" part Bollas likes to call the "me", a "dense inner constellation existing not in the imaginary, but in the real". Who we think we are in relation to the external world, people and objects, and in relation to this part that has no voice though we are aware of it, becomes our "I". This we feel to be our self, and the singer's long-term problem is to become more aware of and therefore in control of self. This awareness under control, guiding toward fuller insight and use of one's potentials, is the underpinning of artistry, the making of expressive sound and visions, movements and stories.

The singer continually asks "who am I?" "What is this all about?" Bollas, in *Cracking Up* has an informative chapter on "What Is This Thing Called Self?" The singer would probably not be able to explain this growth of understanding to others, but it will surely be shown in his behavior, on stage and off.

So how do we become more aware of this self, to be more confident of who and what we are? We will never get rid of some unsureness, and we certainly cannot fulfill all of our potentialities, but with courage (another good C) we can grow. Facing up to external events that shake us is necessary, because not dealing with them tears down confidence. It is equally necessary to deal with hard memories that have been ignored. Sometimes a major experience, and sometimes a seemingly insignificant event, can jar loose a memory that, upon courageous "rational" thought, throws light on a present difficulty. Since our mind and our body never stop working while alive, we have plenty of self experience to process. This does not result in ego-mania, nor the production of divas and divos. Actually, by incorporating more experience and understanding into the ego, the "I" becomes more open and performs its work more easily. After all, Socrates said it long ago: "Know thyself".

What is tricky is that we may approve of one part of our self and have negative thoughts about another part. To gain confidence, one must put together many parts of the self: the part needing relationships, the part needing autonomy, the body self, the cognitive self, the musical self. These must be integrated or brought into a less distracting balance. In another lovely C word, one must center oneself.

I learned how important this concept is when teaching ceramics. First of all, one is working with (mother) Earth. And remember the name Adam means *clay*, so this material has a generative connotation when handled. But before the clay can be drawn up into being a thin-walled pot, it must be centered on the wheel. The ceramics students were universally thrilled when they were able to accomplish the centering, and some of the feeling of being centered grew into their notion of self. Equally, singers must be self-centered (not selfish), integrated in this way. They cannot portray another character if their own is fractured.

The singer, having basically an introverted personality, can more easily pay attention to and try to understand his condensed inner world. This is the world he sings about, and the greater his awareness, the greater his gift in song.

CONCENTRATION

The good singer absolutely cannot be scatter-brained. During training years he must be able to draw together his feel for the correct technique, and concentrate closely on the song's meanings. Add to these the focus needed for memorizing. Then he must bring all his efforts and faculties to bear on performing.

A story in the *Aramco World* (May/June 2000) gives a prime

example of a Mid-Eastern parallel to this Western concentrated work. The story is about Hajjah Maria Ulfah, a great reciter of the Qur'an in Indonesia. Such reciting is not speech-like, but is a combination of chant and song. Hajjah Maria explains that, since the time of Muhammad, there have been passed down seven recitations which can be recited in five different modes suited to various places, occasions, moods. About one in a million or many more of these reciters becomes famous. Hajjah Maria is one of these.

The training includes, of course. being able to read Arabic, often as a second language. The reciter must understand the meaning of every sentence, and match the style to it. Each recitation has its unique mood, flourishes, tempo, pitch, vocal color and duration of certain notes and pauses. Memorizing the whole Qu'ran can be done four pages a day for four years. Some memorize faster.

The *Aramco* article makes clear what is the result of such intense study on the reciter's personality. It describes Hajjah Maria as having a character "at once joyful and intensely focused, authoritative but with humility". The sound of her chant-song parallels the artistry of great western singers.

How is such concentration achieved? Jennifer Larmore says *(Opera News*, July 1998): "Good critics know how really hard it is for a singer to rehearse every day, prepare a score inch by inch, and go through endless rehearsals to come out exhausted, only to have to prepare again to get on stage and deliver it to an audience". The concentration needed to accomplish this is reached with difficulty and hard work.

The singer must find the C-Zone of confidence, commitment, control underlying peak performance. The difference between C-Zoners and others is that they love what they do, and therefore can "get into it" over and over. They have coped with good and bad stress, learned relaxation techniques, and have, by "awfulizing", pushed away the likely happening of the worst possible career situations, distractions, and errors.

Another element in reaching the C-Zone concentration is the courage to take risks—not foolish ones, but those that might pay off in the career, or in personal development. Sometimes the risk would be, for the sake of either preparation or maturation time, to do *less* than the most tempting role choice of the moment. Sometimes the risk would be to make a great leap ahead. Risk-taking is part of the singer's need to control the growth of his career.

Singers may have a late start in training compared to other musicians, but the brains of those who began some instrumental training earlier have already been structured in ways that work well musically. Experiments by Don Hodges and colleagues, at the University of Texas-San Antonio, looked at areas of the brain that were activated when trained musicians played Bach. They found that large areas of the brain were deactivated in performance, indicating extreme concentration. When they asked the musicians to detect errors in a performance of Bach, the imaging showed that the brain areas that process harmony, melody and rhythm are widely dispersed—not as formerly thought in the right brain only.

Neuroscientist Lawrence Parsons, working with the Texas group, was intrigued by the concentration of music activity in the cerebellum, and what that might mean about the cerebellum's function *(Music of the Mind, BBC Music Magazine,* June 2000). In due time, we will be learning more from this research about how the brain runs the show.

Another factor in the singer's reaching this concentration level in work is how well he stays organized in daily life, practice, learning music, travel, plans for performance. Again, being at loose ends will not work. *Classical Singer* magazine, (May 1999) has some good suggestions for smoother care of necessary details. These include having a bank pay bills when you are on the road; entering addresses, appointments, your calendar in a computer program; scheduling health care appointments; using e-mail to stay in touch with your manager; getting your file cabinet organized so your professional papers and resources are in order.

Attention-focusing begins with a bodily felt inner sense (something like the "gut feeling" that is somehow related to intuition). For the moment this allows the singer to unhook his attention from all the outer world pressures and sensory data coming in, and to pay close attention to his inner world, body/mind thoughts and emotions related to the specific on-or-off-stage task at hand.

This requires mental toughness. The book by Lawrence Miller reports on the work of health psychologist Richard Dienstbier of the University of Nebraska, who describes the toughness system. There are two patterns of response to stress. The first sympathetic nervous system response is the hypothalamus acting through the adrenal gland which releases adrenaline. The second system also begins with the hypothalamus but acts through the pituitary gland, which stimulates the adrenal cortex to release cortisol. Together the patterns of these two responses define the nature of the toughness trait.

Dienstbier reports that in tough people the everyday level of activity in the two systems is low, so the person is ordinarily at ease with his circumstances, and his physiological responses reflect this. But when a challenge or a threat brings stress, the first (adrenaline) system kicks up rapidly but the second (cortisol) system remains more stable. When the emergency or problem is met, the adrenaline response drops quickly to normal. In the non-tough psyche, both adrenaline and cortisol remain higher and longer in the nervous system. This results in a more disorganized arousal, less effective coping, which may cause feelings of helplessness or depression.

The coping tough mind gives the singer the confidence that he can meet challenges. So if the singer learns coping skills, his confidence and control at the psychological level will affect his physiological reaction, as we have seen. Part of this coping is imagining alternative solutions and how to work them out. Further, toughness strengthens the immune system, so the singer is also defending against infections and colds.

Shirlee Emmons and psychologist Alma Thomas in *Power*

Performance for Singers, give a thorough definition of mental toughness. They describe a four-stage success process for becoming mentally tough. The first is self-discipline, to be totally dedicated to one's art. This leads to self-control of practice, of behavior, of thinking. Thought then leads to fruitful action. Being totally in control of self and performance brings self-confidence, and this leads to fuller self-realization. The singer can push boundaries that held him back.

This self-understanding, with a less judgmental attitude toward both self and others, means that one's abilities and strengths are there to command. Singing must become easy, but on stage the body must be involved at all times, and the concentration this takes is enormous.

Add physical strength to mental toughness by building an energy reserve through sleep, diet, relaxation, exercise and humor, and you will have the best emotional state for performance.

Concentration is especially needed and too often neglected in practice sessions. Close attention to the score, both words and music, will allow singing it with few mistakes. This kind of attention includes a sense of play, sense of humor, and a letting-go of "should" pressured correctness. If our attention wanders, and we are distracted, we will not even notice making mistakes, and these will carry over into performance. Concentrated playful practice brings concentrated spontaneous production.

Focusing, mindfulness, concentration is something to be learned. The more you practice it, the better it gets. Learning it should be part of voice lessons. Voice teachers may quietly say "concentrate" at an appropriate moment.

There is a good story about a famous baseball pitcher who really worked on his concentration. He said that on his game day, he "put on his game face" early in the morning ("I am confident", "I see the strike zone"). When his wife saw that face, she said, "Oh, yes, this is your holy day!". And his attention and devotion paid off. When concentrated, he saw the strike zone as huge and he could easily control where he put the ball. When not concentrated, the strike zone was so small he couldn't find it. May singers, too, have "holy days".

CONSISTENCY

Another absolute requirement for a professional singer is the ability to present every performance at a consistently satisfactory level. Alternating peak performances with inadequate ones will not extend a career. Confidence strengthens the ability to concentrate. Concentration builds new confidence. With enough confidence, enough concentration, the singer attains consistency, always providing the basic technique is true, and the vocal part has been worked "into the voice". This is where perseverance and patience pay off.

So many skills contribute to consistency. We have already mentioned how necessary it is to concentrate in practice on correctly reading the notes, the rhythm, the words' meaning and diction, the tempo, the expressive marks. This is not perfectionism. It is simply doing what the composer wanted, and if learned in this way, each performance will be on a correct level. This correctness also removes the bumps of tiny unsure hesitations, and keeps the composer's flow and the singer's musical rhythm. My friend Ryan Allen says "there is an old rule of thumb on learning a phrase. It is not learned until you can repeat it three times in a row without a mistake".

Many elements we have already seen as part of the singer's psychology contribute to this almost unending growth of artistry. One is the ability to cut out interfering body tensions and mindless fears, to stay loose, with balanced poise, ease. Athletes say it is not performing well that makes you feel great; it is feeling great that makes you perform well.

Another element of consistency is resilience. If a singer feels he is slipping vocally or bodily or in performance, how well and quickly can he bounce back? There are three factors in the answer to this question: his temperament, the quality of his family life, and his sources of support. Hopefully his family is nurturing and supportive. Hopefully his long training has tempered his rebound from difficulties. But very important is that the singer has social skills and uses them to gain supportive friends, teachers, colleagues. These relationships can add strength to his insight into his work, to his initiative and creative abilities, and to his sense of humor concerning his own or others's part in the production.

Since the brain does not process negative information such as "I will not do this thing that causes me to be inconsistent", the singer must give himself a positive direction. "I control my actions. I specifically will do this, and that, to maintain my level of performance".

One more element in the musician's confidence, concentration, and consistency is his hearing. Horst Günter has an excellent discussion of this in his article *Mental Concepts in Singing* based on his presentation to the Second International Congress of Voice Teachers in Philadelphia, 1991.

If the teacher does not have acute hearing, he cannot analyze the student's sounds correctly and he cannot guide him. The teaching process will be a mechanistic trial and error. The student also must have acute hearing and the chance to hear many great singers in order to build, as Günter says, a mental image of the possible best sound for his own voice. He quotes voice researcher Raoul Husson: "With his larynx, man is able to make noises; he speaks and he sings with his brain".

Horst Günter points out that when the singer has achieved this clear mental image of his own best sound, he then has the ability to study or rehearse his songs or stage work by "mute singing". This saves his voice for company rehearsals and for performance. Günter tells how he used "long train rides between concerts to either repeat the program just sung or to learn new music". He says that Dietrich Fischer-Dieskau's mental command of the voice "was so strong that he could record a song given to him that he had never sung before". Perseverance to attain that ability brings consistency.

The singer who wishes to increase his acuity of listening can use the resources at Tomatis Centers in the USA, Canada and abroad. Dr. Alfred Tomatis, the French otolaryngologist, believes that the voice will only produce easily what the ear can hear or wants to hear. He has demonstrated that when listening is enhanced through auditory stimulation at every stage of life, the voice is enriched and freed and one achieves greater control over the instrument. The Tomatis Method teaches that it is the Ear that commands the voice. The word Ear is used in its broadest sense, which means that the entire body is trained to become a listening and responsive organ. The Ear becomes a creative organ not just a passive one. The development of attuned listening is also used in the treatment of learning and communication disorders at these centers. Marvin Keenze, Professor of Voice and Pedagogy at the Westminster Choir College of Rider University, has experienced the training and has assured me that it has been very beneficial to his own singing and teaching awareness. More information on the Tomatis work can be found on the Internet and from contacting Paul Madaule, The Listening Centre, 599 Markham Street, Toronto, Ontario, Canada M6G 21.7, www.listeningcentre.com.

Don Campbell, in *The Roar of Silence*, has also established that toning or making vocal sounds relevant to the person's situation, can have a healing effect on the body/mind, and can increase hearing accuracy.

CREATIVITY

Over and over we have seen that to live richly, to perform fully, some of the experiences, abilities and freedoms of childhood need to be retained by the adult. The child loses his sense of time, and so does the creative artist, unlike the over-scheduled, time-pressured person. The child has many problems to solve for which he has no ready-made solutions. So has the creative artist and scientist. The child takes great pleasure in finding what are for him new solutions, and the pleasure is almost more important than being right. What matters is joy in the work, not perfection.

We are considering how to become an artist who is creative, so we are not concerned here with the mysterious appearance of a creative genius. A singer with dedication can train his creative insight and creative expressiveness. We humans, from childhood on, are learning machines. The problem is not that a person needs to be motivated to be more creative. The problem is for parents, environment, teachers, peers to keep from turning off the natural motivation we have. Since that interference has happened to a great many singers, they need to get some understanding of what creativity is and how to regain and nurture it.

Lucky are those who grew up in a stimulating environment, not just hearing music, but having art works and all kinds of books to explore. If you are to grow up to sing various characters, the more varied and imaginative lives you can call up, the better.

Creativity is not the same as talent. Talent is a natural ability to work with more than average ease in a given domain, be it ice-skating, mathematics, or whatever. Creativity is a process, in which the person starts with whatever abilities he has and goes through a demanding but possible process that raises these abilities to new heights and strengths.

Traditional psychology theorizes that there are five steps in the creative process. First, when a person is immersed in a domain such as music, he finds a challenging problem in the music he wants to sing, upon which he expends conscious thought. Next comes an incubation period, when without his direction his relaxed brain does its own exploring of the music, after which a new insight occurs. At this point comes the "sweat" part of inspiration-perspiration, the hard work of evaluating, elaborating and integrating the new ideas into a performance. And finally then, the results of the process are presented for acceptance to an audience.

Mihaly Czikszentmihaly discusses aspects of this process in

both his *Flow* and *Creativity* books. He goes on to describe (Creativity, p.111) the enjoyment the creative person feels in experiencing this process, and the elements that make it work. When goals are clear, there is immediate feedback as to whether they are being approached. There is a balance between the challenge and the abilities of the singer/actor. Awareness and action become built into each other. Two things disappear: distractions and self-consciousness. There is no worry of failure. One's sense of time becomes distorted, as though it is standing still and you have all the time in the world. And finally, the activity becomes what he calls "autotelic", that is, that it is done purely for the experience of doing it, not for money, or praise, or success.

This whole process of discovery Czikszentmihaly calls "Flow", which is like "being in the Zone". During the experience, there is very little emotional feeling, as a distraction. Only at the end, after the experience, comes a feeling of elation, happiness, joy in the work.

This sense of flow is so important to the singer in performance. We are dreamers, so we can find creative solutions to the challenges of performing our music and living the life-style. To help the singer nudge along his talent and his luck, I have listed several authors in the bibliography who have more analyses of how to raise creativity.

One is John Sloboda, who in editing *Generative Processes In Music, The Psychology of Performance, Improvisation, and Composition,* has laid a broad base for understanding the musician's creativity. Jeff Pressman, in his chapter on *Improvisation, Methods, and Models*, quotes J.P.Guilford's listing of six aptitudes for creative thinking. They are fluency, flexibility, originality, elaboration, redefinition, and sensitivity to problems. Pressman finds that these aptitudes can allow a musician to improvise freely, with novel melodies, tonalities, rhythms occurring unexpectedly in enchanting ways.

It is my strong belief that any singer who tries out improvising, all by himself and away from the stage, will find it a very freeing practice. What happens as you let one sound lead to another is that it becomes ever more spontaneous—no hesitations—you just allow it to sound. There is definitely a feeling of flow, of the breath making the sound, as my teacher Novikova always said. The trained singer will also have a feeling of structure in the successive sounds, even though they are all unplanned. When the unexpected becomes even more unexpected, the improvisation can turn into hilarious fun. Some of this feeling will carry over into performance. Even though performance is totally prepared, it must seem spontaneous to the audience.

For more ideas along these lines we can always turn to Wesley Balk, a gentle man with tremendous thoughts on how to become more creative. In *Performing Power* he describes the three projective modes of expression, which he says are complex tangled human energy systems. They are the auditory mode of speaking and singing, the kinesthetic mode of movement and gesture, and the facial/emotional mode. His advice is to determine which is your major mode, your strongest, and then to find ways of strengthening your other two modes. He promises that you then can play any character, not just modal duplicates of your self. This is true of acting a character, but this should not lead you into singing a part that is wrong for your voice.

Balk carefully explains how to relate expressions by mode and yet not get them entangled and confused. He also points out that two individuals such as teacher and student can communicate most clearly if they use the same projective mode. It is the teacher's place to study the student's mode and use it to give instructions. Thus the teacher needs to be aware of his own favored mode.

Balk also reminds us: "Everything we can do, we learned as a technique while we were children". And one more consideration is that singers fear harming their voices in expressing emotion; but it is repression, not expression, that blocks the voice.

Another classic teacher for the singer is Konstantine Stanislavsky. Experience Byron, in the *Classical Singer* (October

2000), argues that Stanislavsky's work has been partially misunderstood in the United States, but that singers can benefit much by trying out his later psychophysical approach to operatic acting, especially useful in smaller houses. It seems that Stanislavsky was passionate about opera and he thought of the singer "not as a puppet but as an active creator of the drama". Singers should no more manufacture a statement about a character's behavior or emotion than they should manufacture a sound. All the meanings and emotions must not be faked, but done truthfully, so the singer must make choices toward this end. These modal choices need to be tried out, then the ones that work must be practiced.

Like many good teachers and coaches, Stanislavsky started with relaxation, and this is how Fyodor Chaliapin worked, getting rid of distractions and unnecessary physical tensions, to gain the concentration needed for creative work. Dr. Byron gives a good summary of the next steps Stanislavsky worked out. Her book on the Stanislavsky System is forthcoming.

Finally, we must come back to the bottom line for doing creative work: re-thinking and re-integrating ideas, with perseverance over a long time. The very creative dancer/choreographer Twyla Tharp says "you don't get into the mood to create—it is discipline—this is what you do". So if you come into a dry spell, you simply go ahead and work—go through the process again until a new light shines.

CHARISMA

Charisma, a rare quality or power attributed to those persons who have demonstrated an exceptional ability for leadership and for securing the devotion of large numbers of people.

The whole point of all the professional singer's study and preparation of voice and song is to give a charismatic performance, that is, one of beauty, grace and power. I have personally known one such singer. She was Wadeeha Atiyeh, a Lebanese-American who gave full one-woman programs of stories and songs from her Mid-Eastern culture, which she wove into a dramatic sequence. She was charismatic in performance, and to some extent offstage as well, due to her appearance, voice, and manner.

It is not easy to describe charisma, though we surely recognize and respond to it. It is even harder to say what it is, where it comes from. The Indo-European root of the word is Gher, which has various traditional meanings that help define the present word. Gher—to grasp, to enclose (garden). Gher—to call out, greet. Gher—to shine, glow. Gher—to scratch, carve (related to writing a character on stone), to make an impression. Gher—to like, to want. Gher—gut, string.

As I recall Wadeeha's characteristics that affected her audience, a number of adjectives leap to mind: warm, magnetic, energy level rising, amazing grace, full presence, daring freedom, unpredictable, intensely involved, inner harmony, radiance, voice full of life and color. There is a story about the incandescent soprano Leonie Rysanek that makes the main point. A male colleague said, in awe: "When Rysanek is singing fortissimo in your face, you basically just hope that your contact lenses aren't going to melt!"

Charisma is not something we can work for directly. I do believe a singer can become charismatic through devoted work toward the first four C's. With confidence, concentration, consistent and evermore creative performance, the singer becomes more powerful, more expressive, more impressive. He or she lights up the stage.

CODA

The core psychological questions a career singer must be able to answer are:

> What do I have to sing about? This takes imagination.
>
> When I open my mouth, do I know what sound will happen? This needs discipline.

Do I have something true to myself to give? This means accepting one's sound-self.

Do I have confidence both in my ability, and in the beauty and meaning of music? If so, this brings radiance.

Finally, do I see the wonder of the mind, the wonder of language, the wonder of melody, the wonder of the voice?

We have come to the end of this voyage exploring the psychological situation of persons with songs in their psyches. Can you imagine a world without song? We need to sing. We need to hear singing.

Singers can feel both proud and humble of their gift. Singing is an ultimate expression of humanity's living, loving, thinking, striving in this mysterious awesome universe. With all the unity of our physical, musical and psychological strength, let us sing.

—Before enlightenment, chop wood, carry water.
After enlightenment, chop wood, carry water.

—Zen saying

—I am now as I was when I was 20 years old. I was nobody, and I am still nobody. I am a human being like others, and people feel this. Victoria is like us, except she sings.

—Victoria de los Angeles

—A bird does not sing because it has an answer.
It sings because it has a song.

—Chinese proverb

—In bocca al lupo.

—Pre-performance wish

SUPPLEMENT A

PAOLA NOVIKOVA'S STORY
Early Performance, Study, and Teaching Experience

Paola Novikova (1896-1967) was a coloratura soprano, born in Russia, studied in Germany and Italy, who eventually became one of the 20th Century great voice teachers. She was the student of the great baritone Mattia Battistini, so her teaching was traditional Italianate intuitive approach. Dr. Berton Coffin, through whom I found her and studied with her the last two years of her life, has some description of her work in his book *Sounds of Singing* (Scarecrow Press). He also made a descriptive audiotape of her work based on observations of many lessons with her long list of international stars, such as Nicolai Gedda, George London, Helen Donath, etc. He sent me this tape, and there is a copy in the Music Department of the University of Colorado.

The New York Times critic said this of her first New York recital: "Mme. Novikova sings with elegance, taste, and subtlety", and this is precisely the way she helped her students sing, training the voice as an instrument. It was partly due to her example that I came to a fuller understanding of the psychology of singing.

She made an audiotape for her students, describing her early vocal studies. The following transcript of this tape, retaining some of her Russian accent, is given as one singer's trials of performance and of finding a teacher.

PAOLA NOVIKOVA'S EARLY LIFE STORY

I was born on the Volga in the middle of Russia. At the revolution I fled with my parents to Berlin. I was in the 10th grade. I always dreamt to become a singer. As a child I was a clown. I grew up in my grandparent's home. But my grandfather, the old Russian noble, his thoughts of the stage were quite different from now. When he heard me (that I wanted to be a singer) I was left without dessert, I was put in a corner and I simply should not speak about it.

My aunt was one of the great pianists of Russia, but not allowed to pursue a career. She devoted her life to bringing me up, because my mother was ill, unfortunately. Music was part of my life from early ages 4 or 5. Bach, Beethoven, Brahms, Schubert and Schumann were nothing new to me, because 4, 5, 6 hours a day they were played heavenly by my late aunt.

So I moved to Berlin but my first thought was to study singing. But I had no means. We lost everything. But I think I was very fortunate by nature. I was also very lucky to find the right people at the right moment. In Berlin there were a few families who were very fond of me and sponsored my singing lessons.

Unfortunately I studied 4 years, and in 4 years I changed 11 teachers. I mean it—all the greatest teachers of Berlin could not cope with my inquisitive nature, because I always asked "why", and "how" and I never had an answer.

One fine day I felt my voice was disappearing, and I was completely without voice for one year. Then I got a kind of black melancholy. I was sitting at the window not speaking to anyone. I was just desperate. The only thing I wanted in life was to sing. A friend of mine, who won the grandprix of Pleyel, said to me: "What you need now, because we love you what we need now, is to find out: are you really a talent? or just a bluff?". "To find out you have to go on the stage, to sing for an audience, and see how the audience will receive you". Basic, this was what I wanted. My friends offered to sponsor my concert—it cost about 1200 marks or \$300, the equivalent then of \$1000.00. But the basic thing was at that time the audience was so spoiled by the fantastic great artists—they had Elena Gerhardt, Clara Dukes, all the great stars of the world, so they simply refused to go to some kind of debut.

So here again I was broke morally. So my friends said "the only thing to do is find a great accompanist. Maybe the accompanist will be some sort of an attraction. Well, the greatest accompanist was Michael Rauchheisen, maybe the greatest of all time, the equivalent of what Gerald Moore is today. I took my music. I packed it in my briefcase—everything from Rossini to Mahler, Schumann, all kinds. I simply wanted to impress Mr. Rauchheisen. I forgot how hard it is to impress such a colossal as Mr. Reichhausen was. I go to his apartment, I ring the doorbell, I come into his apartment. He looks at me—I was still very little. I am not even five feet, and I didn't grow since then. I had two red braids. But I was full of enthusiasm. That is all that was in me. I think that this was somehow contagious to Mr. Reichhausen.

He looked me up and down—he was about 6'4" and I was less than 5'. "Fräulein, what can I do for you?" "Well, I would like you to play for me at a concert". I don't think he experienced anything like that before, that a nobody came to him and wanted him to play at a concert. He played only for celebrities.

"Oh, no, miss, but that is not possible. I am booked up for the next two years and there is no time". He saw two tears coming up in my eyes, and he said "Would you like to sing for me? Maybe I can give you some kind of advice". And I said, "Yes, I would", and I took out one of the hardest of the repertoire, *Die Mondnacht* by Schumann. It is all sostenuto, mezza voce and PP. Afterwards when I became already a somebody I thought "Should I really do *Die Mondnacht*?" But at that time I put the first thing on the piano and it was *Die Mondnacht*.

Mr. Reichhausen played like a god. I sang less well than a god sings, I think. But I went on with enthusiasm and with a desire to impress him. I was surprised that he shrugged his shoulders the whole time I sang. When I finished he said, "Well, miss, I never experienced such a thing. Whatever you do is wrong. Your breath control is wrong, Your style is wrong. One note is heavenly and the next tone is atrocious. Your way of singing is absolutely unacceptable. But it is very fascinating the way you do such things. Well, I will help you. I will play for you". I embraced him and gave him a big kiss and thanked him. Then asked him: "It is a problem what I should do". "Oh", he said, "it doesn't matter what you do—whatever it is it is wrong. So you just pick the things you like".

I said "I would like to do *Il Re Pastore* by Mozart to start. "Okey", he said. Now I am sure you know *Il Re Pastore* is one of the hardest things for a soprano to sing. She has seven pages, all those things, and then one page of cadenza, unaccompanied. It is one of the hardest tasks a singer has in the repertoire. But I was so ignorant and so enthusiastic about myself and about the chances opening for me that I decided to start with *Il Re Pastore*.

Mr. Reichhausen got up from his chair and went to the telephone. He calls up Joseph Volkstein who was the first violinist in the Berlin Philharmonic. What he says to him: "I have here a little Russian. She is a very strange creature, but something very fascinating. I am going to play for her concert. Would you like to take over the obligato for *Il Re Pastore*? Joseph Volkstein, knowing how Reichhausen played, said yes. So my concert had two of the greatest collaborators that an artist could wish for.

Now about that Beckstein concert, I must unfortunately confess it was the greatest fiasco of my life. Fortunately it was the only fiasco, but big enough to last my lifetime. The audience loved me, I don't know why. I think because of my enthusiasm, because of my youth, because of my joy of singing, because of my linguistic talent, perhaps because of a special quality of my voice.

But the critics in all countries are the same. Berlin at that time had 14 newspapers. The next day all 14 newspapers told that I was so courageous to invite all those people to the Beckstein

Saal to show how it shouldn't be done. Everybody of the critics still recognized certain qualities in me. Somebody found a very beautiful voice, or a great interpretive talent, or some kind of familiarity of expression, etc. But all in all the criticisms were atrocious, and I should have forgotten to sing and have a career. But as I told you I always was very lucky. When the audience was applauding and the ladies who sponsored my concert were very proud of me, and said "do you see, you will be a world celebrity. Tomorrow will come the papers and Paolinchka will be known all over the world".

Suddenly I see a very tall, very elegant gentleman, who introduces himself. He was nobody else but Mattia Battistini. I had the great fortune that Battistini at that time was in Berlin for his own recital. My great maestro used to come five days before the recital to get used to the climate, to the water, food.

Unfortunately our artists of today take a different approach to singing. They sing today in Texas, tomorrow in Atlantic City, and this is what wears them and by the age of 40, the sound already is as if they were 70, and my maestro sang until he was 69. I heard him at the age of 69.

He introduced himself and he was very kind at the beginning. He said all the nice things about me. The inborn poise, the musicality, all those things. And then he said, "But why don't you study singing, for pity's sake? Your singing is below any criticism. You have no idea about breath control, no idea about diction—just no idea about singing".

I started crying very bitterly, and I said, "Well, maybe I don't understand, maybe I have no talent. For four years, I changed 11 teachers. I even lost my voice. I simply did not succeed. I don't know what it means".

To make a long story short, Maestro Battistini was generous. He took me with him to Italy, and I am one of the most fortunate people on earth. I had the great luck to have the great master who has never been surpassed. Nobody surpassed Battistini, and when I asked him "why" and "when" he was certainly capable to answer all those questions. I drank as much as I could of that divine knowledge that he poured into me, and I became what I became because I am very fortunate.

(Man's voice on the tape): "Then he had very few pupils?"

Paola: "had no pupils".

Man: "You were his only pupil?"

Paola: "only".

Man: "Did it take a bit of persuasion?"

Paola: He never took pupils. I attended once at a very comical meeting. He used to live out of town from Rome. He had a villa, and in his whole living room which was about twice the size of my studio, there was no wallpaper, there was only the ribbons of the flowers he got at his appearances. And all of a sudden the butler comes in and announces an American gentleman who wants to speak to him. The gentleman comes in, very nice, very plain, and says "Maestro Battistini, I would like to sing the way you do. How much do I have to pay?"

This was a little bit an antique American approach to things. And Battistini said, "I never give lessons", and he never did. Now and then, if some of the colleagues came and asked him for advice, he gave some advice. He said that you have something in the middle register, or you are pushing the high notes, or the low register is off pitch or your breath control is wrong. He never gave lessons. He gave lessons to me because of that extreme luck. (The luck was that Battistini had stayed at her home during his recitals in Russia, and at age 7 she had sat on his lap, so that later he recognized her).

You have to be lucky in life, no matter how talented you are. If you are not fortunate you cannot make anything, this is my firm belief. Battistini was idolized in Russia. My grandfather was a governor when I grew up, and when Battistini used to come to Russia, the grandfather said "The best for him, the best sleigh in winter". Battistini used to live in our home 3-4-5 days, treated as a king, with silver trays, silver samovars or whatever he wanted. Then, Battistini when he saw me, and saw me crying so much, because after the concert I was supposed to come to him at the hotel, and bring the newspapers, and he was sitting in the hall, waiting for me with all the newspapers that he read. He was already au courant what kind of a "triumph" it was. I think if the rugs of that hotel exist, they still must be wet from the tears I cried in that hall, from what Battistini said to me and how he spoke to me. In the end he asked me "Tell me, who *are* you? Where are you coming from?" And he remembered that he always saw a little girl in the studio of my grandfather, and somewhere sitting on the lap of Battistini. I was at that time 7 years. I could give myself that kind of luxury. Doesn't it seem like a fairy tale? But it is true.

(Man's voice): "And how many years were you with him?"

Paola: It was unfortunately very short. He died after eight months".

BUT, just to imitate him for one week is equivalent of years of study. It was such an impeccable way of singing. And such a great knowledge. And he was such a great personality. And such a great gentleman. And I owed my whole life practically to him.

But, before he died he tried out my pedagogical capacities. Because he said to me, "Child, the old bel canto style is dying out. Maybe there will come a day when you will be the only representative of the bel canto. We have to keep it alive". And this was the end of the conversation.

One day a lady from Helsinki, Finland, came to my very modest room and she said to me "You have to help me, to get back the contract. I sang Tosca and I broke two consecutive evenings the B-flat in "Vissi d'arte". I took the train and I went to Battistini and he told me he doesn't give lessons but he has a little Russian protegé and I should come to you".

I was scared stiff. I almost died. I didn't know where to start. I didn't know what teaching means. I started teaching that poor singer. I told her the best I could. I showed her the way I inhaled, the way I formed my mask, what the resonators are, what the diction is, and I worked with her two and three times a day. I almost killed her, because I didn't know any better.

And what do you think? After six weeks of this kind of torture she went back to Helsinki, sang "Cieli ozzuri", Aida's second aria, attacked the C natural on PP, made a crescendo on it, brought it back to pp, received back her contract, called up Battistini begging him to convince me to come to Helsinki to start a school of teaching. But I wanted to sing myself. And this is the way my great master discovered in me the pedagogical talent. It is no credit to me—I am just born with it. This is why I speak about it so frankly. I don't know how I form my great celebrities, George London, Nicolai Gedda. I worked with Hilda Guedon, Hilda Zadek, Erich Kunz, all these are quite names. Why they came to me I don't know. How I taught them, I don't know.

To get the wrong teacher is a tragedy. I don't think now of the money the student loses, it is the time he loses. I had dozens and dozens of people who came to me for auditions, who were morally absolutely destroyed because they did not succeed in their singing. And when I told them "But you have all the credentials for becoming a serious singer. What you have to do is just to find the right teacher".

Singing is not a mystery, it is a science, and the instrumentalist has to know the positions. The same way, we singers have to know the position of our resonators, of our breath, which is the main factor in singing. Everybody trains the voice, they forget the voice is a consequence. How can I train the consequence? I have to train the cause.

—Donna Paola Novikova

SUPPLEMENT B

RESOURCES FOR CAREER PLANNING

BOOKS

Shirlee Emmons and Alma Thomas: *Power Performance for Singers, Transcending the Barriers,* 1998. Oxford University Press, New York.
A very thorough and psychologically oriented analysis of Preperformance, Performance, and Postperformance elements, which yield performance power.

Janis Papolos: *The Performing Artist's HANDBOOK.* 1984. Writer's Digest Books, Cincinnati, OH.
Information that does not become obsolete on resumés, photographs, professional polish, unions, audio and video demos, managers, publicity, networking, business, and a list of services. Her performance checklist includes "emergency sewing repair kit"!

CLASSICAL SINGER (magazine). P.O. Box 95490. South Jordan, UT 84095-0490.
Lists auditions, competitions, online voice teacher, online performance, online singer directories. Mental health, real

life, money, performance reviews, summer programs, vocal health.

HAGEGARDEN (reported in Opera News, Jan '96, p. 23).

A Swedish retreat established by Hakan Hagegard, where performing artists can go for rehearsing and recreation in a natural creative environment. Hagegarden has also set up "fiberoptics and a computer superhighway" over which singers can audition for opera houses and concert series all around the world. This system can even simulate the acoustics of individual halls.

NATIONAL ASSOCIATION OF TEACHERS OF SINGING

Executive Director, 6406 Merrill Road, Jacksonville, FL 32277.

Journal of Singing, list of NATS teachers, NATS auditions, workshops.

GUIDE TO THE NATIONAL ENDOWMENT FOR THE ARTS, available from the Office of Public Affairs, The National Endowment for the Arts, 1100 Pennsylvania Ave., N.W., Washington, DC 20506. Publishes *Foundation Grants to Individuals*.

OPERA AMERICA, 1156 15th St.N.W. Suite 910, Washington, DC 20005-1704

Career Guide for Singers, 5th ed. Lists producing organizations, institutes, workshops, competitions, grants, artist managers, and gives data on auditions.

Business Advice for Singers.

Audition Advice for Singers. Write for membership information.

STATE and REGIONAL ARTS COUNCILS offer residencies and performances.

SUPPLEMENT C

MOVEMENT ARTS

Restorative of Mind/Body Balance

Movement arts may be generally viewed as part of the technique of singing. They are that, but even more they are the underpinning of psychological well-being. They induce (not impose) a balanced supportive body alignment, a feeling both of being "grounded" and being "up", a restoration of ready energy, a depth of breathing. All this contributes to a gracefully efficient body and a calm, concentrated mind.

The article and books first listed are not the most recent ones discussing movement arts in general and particular, but they are some of the clearest and wisest.

Miller, Richard: The Wisdom of the Body in Singing. The NATS Journal, Jan/Feb 1990, 20.

Borysenko, Joan (1987): Minding the Body, Mending the Mind. Reading, MA, Addison-Wesley Publishing Co.

Goleman, Daniel, & Bennett-Goleman, Tara (1986): The Relaxed Body Book. New York, Doubleday.

Lidell, Lucy (1987): The Sensual Body. New York, Simon and Schuster.

ALEXANDER TECHNIQUE

The Alexander Technique was developed by Australian actor F.M. Alexander to solve his own vocal problems. He discovered that the relation of the head, neck, and spine is crucial in determining quality of movement and of vocal function. When the neck muscles do not over-work, the head balances lightly and the spine naturally lengthens. The whole body's support system works. For the singer/actor this brings a gain in ease of movement, breathing, timing, and expressiveness. Awareness is the key word. The Technique is a re-education, concerned with the whole self, the mind/body, and how we use it.

AmSAT (The American Society for the Alexander Technique).
PO Box 60008, Florence, MA 01062
List of books and articles on Alexander Technique is available from AmSAT. List of certified A.T. teachers in North America, as well as general information.

www.alexandertechnique.com/singers

REFERENCES

Alexander, F.M. (1984). The Use of the Self. Downey, CA, Centerline Press.

Conable, B. & Conable, W. (1992): How to Learn the Alexander Technique, A Manual for Students. Columbus, OH, Andover Road Press.

DeAlcantara, P. (1997): Indirect Procedures, A Musician's Guide to the Alexander Technique. Oxford, Oxford University Press.

Duarte, F.: The Principles of the Alexander Technique Applied to Singing: The Significance of the Preparatory Set.
Journal of Research in Singing, Vol. 5, 1, Dec 1981, 3-21.

Farkas, Alexander: Alexander and Voice. The NATS Journal, March/April 1994, 15-18.

Gelb, Michael (1987): Body Learning: An Introduction to the

Alexander Technique. New York, Henry Holt & Co.

Heirich, Jane R.: The Alexander Technique and Voice Pedagogy. The NATS Journal, May/June 1993, 16-19.

Valentine, E.R., Fitzgerald, D., Gorton, T., Hudson, J., Symonds, E.: The Effect of Lessons in the Alexander Technique on Music Performance in High and Low Stress Situations. Psychology of Music, 1995, 23, 129-141.

Zipperer, D.: The Alexander Technique as a Supplement to Voice Production. Journal of Research in Singing, XIV, 2, June 1991, 1-40.

HERBERT BENSON—RELAXATION RESPONSE

Dr. Herbert Benson, of the Harvard Medical School and Director of the Hypertension Section of Boston's Beth Israel Hospital, developed his Relaxation Response after he noticed the good effects obtained in meditation. This Response is easily learned, costs nothing, and has no side effects. This, of course, is not a "movement" art, but I must include it as an excellent practice for releasing stress tensions. It can also, due to its focus, bring about a higher level of self-acceptance and insight about oneself.

Benson, Herbert & Kipper, Miriam (1976): The Relaxation Response. New York, Aeon Books.

Benson, Herbert (1979): The Mind/Body Effect. New York, Simon & Schuster.

Benson, Herbert & Proctor, William (1985): Beyond the Relaxation Response. New York, Berkley.

DALCROZE EURYTHMICS

"Mind and body form a perfect instrument whereon to learn to play the song of life". So Dalcroze said, and his work aims at obtaining for the musician the utmost benefit of the faculties he already possesses. Plato long ago noted that "Rhythm, i.e., the expression of order and symmetry, penetrates by way of the body into the soul and into the entire man, revealing to him the harmony of his whole personality". And Pierre Bernac points out that singers often have a tendency to make what he calls "involuntary nuances", varying the intensity and rhythm of sound in their vocal line without any expressive or musical reason. Whereas, a whole phrase or whole page of music without any involuntary change of dynamics can be so beautiful.

Dalcroze Eurythmics addresses these needs of connecting body/mind rhythms and music, and provide a musical learning experience involving movement, the ear, feeling, technique, and expression.

Dalcroze School of Music, 129 West 67th St., New York, NY 10023-5915.

Abramson, Robert (1974): Rhythm Games for Perception and Cognition. Book and set of two tapes. New York, Music and Movement Press.

Jacques-Dalcroze, Emile (1967): Rhythm, Music and Education. (trans. Harold F. Robenstein). Redcourt, England, The Dalcroze Society, Inc.

Choksy, L., Abramson, R., Gillespie, A., Woods, D. (1986): Teaching Music in the Twentieth Century. New Jersey, Prentice-Hall.

FELDENKRAIS AWARENESS THROUGH MOVEMENT

Feldenkrais work has two basic forms: Functional Integration, a gentle body manipulation, and Awareness Through Movement (ATM), an exercise that can later become self-directed into endless movement improvisations. It becomes a re-learning process, with attention directed to the fine details of slow, gentle movement, and directed at creating changes in the nervous system.

www.feldendrais.com

Feldenkrais Guild of North America. 3611 SW Hood Avenue, Suite 100, Portland, OR 97201. Phone (800)775-2118.

REFERENCES

Arnold, Judy: The Feldenkrais Method: Awareness Through Movement. The Delta Kappa Gamma Bulletin, Summer 1991, 29-35.

Feldenkrais, Moshe (1972): Awareness Through Movement. New York, Harper & Row.

Rywerant, Yochanan (1983): The Feldenkrais Method, Teaching by Handling. New York, Harper & Row.

Spire, Mary: The Feldenkrais Method: An Interview with Anat Baniel. Medical Problems of Performing Artists, Dec 1989, 159-162.

T'AI CHI CH'UAN

T'ai Chi is meditation in motion. There are forms to learn, but everyone can do the slow, fluid movements. The aim is the coordination of mind and body. It emphasizes slow breathing, a series of moving balanced and relaxed postures derived from the natural stances of animals, and a calmness of mind. The Chinese say that those who do T'ai Chi correctly for a few minutes twice a day will gain the pliability of a child, the health of a lumberjack, and the peace of mind of a sage.

VIDEOS

T'ai Chi for Health, Yang Short Form/Yang Long Form. Each form 120 min. Interarts Production. Available through the SelfCare Catalog, (Emeryville, CA), Phone (800)345-3371.

Yang Short Form Style T'ai Chi, 107 min. Patience T'ai Chi Association, Phone (718)332-3477.

BOOKS

The Teachings of Master T.T.Liang; compiled by Stuart Alve Olson, (1992). Imagination Becomes Reality—T'ai Chi Ch'uan, A Complete Guide to the 150 Posture Solo Form. Dragon Door Publications, inc., PO Box 4381, St. Paul, MN 55104. Phone (612)645-0517.

Chungliang Al Huang (1988): Embrace Tiger, Return to Mountain; The Essence of T'ai Chi. Celestial Arts. Phone (800)841-2665.

TRAGER PSYCHOPHYSICAL INTEGRATION with MENTASTICS

Trager Psychophysical Integration is the innovative approach to movement re-education developed by Milton Trager, M.D., at first in connection with his medical practice. After retirement, he devoted full time to research, writing, and training practitioners and instructors throughout the world. The Trager work on the body for at least an hour is gentle and rhythmical, so clients experience the possibility of being able to move that freely, effortlessly and gracefully on their own. The exercises following the experience are called Mentastics, not gymnastics. They are mindfulness in motion.

www.trager.com (Trager Institute).

Trager, Milton, with Cathy Guadagno (1987): Trager Mentastics, Movement as a Way to Agelessness. Barryton, NY, Station Hill Press, Inc.

YOGA

Yoga is a mind/body practice that involves movement through physical poses, called asanas. A basic element of yoga is the connection of body and breath with brain. One branch requires greater physical work, another focuses on alignment. The most common versions in the US are Kundalini yoga, or Hatha yoga, with attention on the breath. The poses stretch muscles and lengthen the spine. The slow deep breath induced is a great plus in a singer's preparation.

www.yrec.org	Yoga Research and Education, CA
www.yogajournal.com	The Yoga Journal, CA
www.yogasito.com	State by state listing of Yoga teachers.
www.yogadirectory.com	Links to websites of teachers, centers, and retreats.

VIDEO
Yoga Basics, a Beginner's Class, with Lindsay Clennell. Psychology Today Video, 49 East 21st St. 11th floor, New York, NY 10010

BOOKS
Schaeffer, Rachel (1998): Yoga for Your Spiritual Muscles. Quest Books

Winding, Eleanor (1982): Yoga for Musicians, and Other Special People. Sherman Oaks, CA, Alfred Publishing Co.

Yoga International (magazine). R.R. 1, Box 407, Honesdale, PA 18431.

BIBLIOGRAPHY

Acoustics/Resonance

Benade, A.H. (1976). Fundamentals of Musical Acoustics. New York, Oxford University Press.

Coffin, B. (1980). Overtones of Bel Canto: Phonetic Basis of Artistic Singing. Metuchen, N.J., Scarecrow Press.

Miller, R. (1997). Throat Sensation During Singing. The NATS Journal of Singing, Mar/April, 33-34.

Titze, I. (1999). Natural Frequencies in Our Bodies. Journal Of Singing, 55(5), 27-29. Philadelphia, the Voice Foundation.

Tsur, R. (1992). What Makes Sound Patterns Expressive? The Poetic Mode of Speech Perception. Durham, Duke University Press.

Winkel, F. (1967). Music, Sound and Sensation. New York, Dover.

Adolescence

Bleiberg, E. (1988). Adolescence, Sense of Self, and Narcissistic Vulnerability. Bulletin of the Menninger Clinic, 52(3), 211-229.

Brigham, T.A. (1989). Self-management for Adolescents: A Skills Training Program. New York, Guilford Press.

Powells, R.M. (1983). The Changing Voice: A Vocal Chameleon. The Choral Journal, Sept, 11-17.

Menninger, W.W. (1988). The Crisis of Adolescence and Aging. Bulletin of the Menninger Clinic, 52(3).

Sataloff, R.T. (1989). The Young Voice. The NATS Journal, Jan/Feb, 35-37.

Sugar, M. (1993). Female Adolescent Development. New York, Brunner/Mazel.

Wexler, D.B. (1991). The Adolescent Self. New York, W.W. Norton.

Body Messages

Bean, M. (1998). Gesture in Art Song and Opera. The NATS Journal of Singing, May/June, 37-39.

Kramer, S. & Akhtar, S. (1992). When the Body Speaks: Psychological Meanings in Kinetic Clues. Northvale, N.J., Jacob Aronson.

Landau, T. (1989). About Faces, Evolution of the Human Face, Why It Mirrors the Mind. New York, Doubleday Dell Publishing Group.

Langs, R.J. (1983). Unconscious Communication In Everyday Life. New York, Jacob Aronson.

Levasseur, S. (1995). Nonverbal Communication in the Applied Voice Studio. Journal of Research in Singing, 18(2).

Marsh, P. (1988). Eye to Eye, How People Interact. Topsfield, MA, Salem House Publishers.

Morris, D. (1985). Body Watching, A Field Guide to the Human Species. New York, Crown Publishers Inc.

Nix, J. (1998). "Dear Diary", Body Monitoring Techniques for Singers. The NATS Journal of Singing, March/April, 25-29.

Pierce, A. & Pierce, R. (1989). Expressive Movement, in Daily Life, Sports and the Performing Arts. New York, Plenum Press.

Pierce, A. & Pierce, R. (1991). A Practical Guide to Balance in Action. Redlands, CA, Center of Balance Press.

Pisk, L. (1976). The Actor and His Body. New York, Theatre Arts Books.

Sabatine, J. (1983). The Actor's Image, Movement Training for Stage and Screen. New Jersey, Prentice-Hall.

Schneider, S.K. (1994). Concert Song as Seen: Kinesthetic Aspects of Musical Interpretations. Stuyvesant, NY, Pendragon Press.

Body/Mind, Movement, Stage Training

Balk, W. (1977). The Complete Singer-Actor: Training for Music Theater. Minneapolis, University of Minnesota Press.

Benson, H. (1975). The Relaxation Response. New York, Morrow.

Bermúdez, J.L., Marcel, A.J., & Eilan, N. (1995). The Body and the Self. Cambridge MA, MIT Press.

Byron, E. (2000). Stanislavsky and the Classical Singer. Classical Singer, 13(10), 10-21.

Choksy, L., Abramson, R., Gillespie, G., & Woods, D. (1986). The Approach of Emile Jaques-Dalcroze, Chapter 3 in Teaching Music in the Twentieth Century, on Movement, Rhythm, and Improvisation, 27-69.

DeAlcantara, P. (1997). Indirect Procedures, A Musician's Guide to the Alexander Technique. Oxford, Oxford University Press.

Edwin, R. (1992). The Bach to Rock Connection: The Language of a Body. The NATS Journal March/April, 37-38.

Feldenkrais, M. (1977). Awareness Through Movement (illus.ed.). New York, Harper and Row.

Galway, T. (1979). The Inner Game of Tennis. New York, Bantam Books.

Garner, S.B. (1994). Bodied Spaces, Phenomenology and Performance in Contemporary Drama. Ithaca/London, Cornell University Press.

Goldovsky, B. (1968). Bringing Opera To Life; Operatic Acting and Stage Direction. New York: Appleton-Century-Crofts.

Green, B. & Gallway, T. (1986). The Inner Game of Music. Garden City, NY, Anchor Press/Doubleday.

Harré, E. (1994). Physical Being, a Theory for a Corporeal Psychology. Oxford, Blackwell Publications.

Jacobsen, E. (1974). Progressive Muscular Relaxation. Chicago, the University of Chicago Press, Midway Reprint.

Johnson, M. (1987). The Body in the Mind, The Bodily Basis of Meaning, Imagination, and Reason. Chicago, University of Chicago Press.

Kepner, J.I. (1993). Body Process: Working with the Body in Psychotherapy. A Gestalt Institute of Cleveland Publication.

Miller, R. (1990). The Wisdom of the Body in Singing. The NATS Journal, Jan/Feb, 20-21.

Munro, M. & Larson, M. (1996). The Influence of Body Integration on Voice Production. Journal of Singing, Nov/Dec, 17-24.

Natelson, B. (1999). Facing and Fighting Fatigue. New Haven, Yale University Press.

Ohrenstein, D. (1999). Physical Tension, Awareness Techniques, and Singing. Journal of Singing, Sept.Oct. 23-27.

Rubin, L.S. (1980). Movement for the Actor. New York, Drama Book Specialists.

Titze, I. (1997). Control of Movement in One's Body. Journal of Singing, March/April, 33-34.

Whitfield, P. (1995). The Human Body Explained. New York, Henry Holt.

Brain and Musical Brain

Butler, G. & Hope, T. (1995). Managing Your Mind. New York, Oxford University Press.

Campbell, D. (1983). Introduction to the Musical Brain. Saint Louis, MO, Magnamusic-Baton.

Damasio, A.R. (1994). Descartes' Error: Emotion, Reason, and the Human Brain. New York, G.P. Putnam.

DeCuevas, J. (1994). Mind, Brain, Behavior. Harvard Magazine, Nov/Dec, 36-43.

Dowling, W.J., & Harwood, D.L. (1986). Music Cognition. Orlando, Academic Press.

Edelman, G.M. (1989). The Remembered Present: A Biological

Theory of Consciousness. New York, Basic Books.

Fields, V.A. (1972). How Mind Governs Voice. The NATS Bulletin, Dec, 2-10.

Gazzaniga, M.S. (1988). Mind Matters, How the Mind and Brain Interact to Create Our Conscious Lives. Boston, Houghton Mifflin.

Gazzaniga, M.S. & Bizzi, E. (2000). The New Cognitive Neurosciences, (2nd ed.). Cambridge MA, MIT Press.

Jourdain, R. (1997). Music, the Brain, and Ecstasy. New York, William Morrow & Co.

Langer, E.J. (1989) Mindfulness. Reading, MA, Addison-Wesley.

Lazarus, A.L. (1984). In the Mind's Eye, The Power of Imagery for Personal Nnrichment. New York, Guilford Press.

Lederman, R.J. (1998). Neurological Problems of Performing Artists. In R.T. Sataloff, A.G. Brandfonbrener, & R.J. Lederman (eds.), Performing Arts Medicine (2nd ed.). San Diego CA, Singular Publishing Co.

Leonard, J. (1999). The Sorcerer's Apprentice, Unlocking Secrets of the Brain's Basement. Harvard Magazine, May/June, 15-18.

Ornstein, R.E. (1990). The Healing Brain, a Scientific Reader. New York, Guilford Press.

Ornstein, R.E. (1997). The Right Mind: Making Sense of the Hemispheres. New York, Harcourt Brace.

Penrose, R. (1989). The Emperor's New Mind, Concerning Computers, Minds, and the Laws of Physics. Oxford, Oxford University Press.

Reiser, M.F. (1984). Mind, Brain, Body: Toward a Convergence of Psychoanalysis and Neurobiology. New York, Basic Books.

Restak, R.M. (1988). The Mind. Toronto, New York, Bantam Books.

Rutter, M. & Rutter, M. (1993). Developing Minds. New York, Basic Books, Harper Collins.

Siegel, D.J. (1999). The Developing Mind: Toward a Neurobiology of Interpersonal Experience. New York, Guilford Press.

Storr, A. (1992). Music and the Mind. New York, Macmillan.

Wilson, E.O. (1998). Consilience, The Unity of Knowledge. New York, Alfred A. Knopf.

Breathing

Leanderson, R. & Sundberg, J. (1988). Breathing for Singing. Journal of Voice (2)1, 2-12. Philadelphia, The Voice Foundation.

Proctor, D.F. (1980). Breathing, Speech and Song. Wien, New York, Springer-Verlag.

Wormhoudt, P.S. (1981). Building the Voice as an Instrument. Oskaloosa, IA, William Penn College.

Career

Davis, P.G. (1997). The American Opera Singer, the Lives and Adventures of America's Great Singers in Opera and Concert, from 1825 to the Present. New York, Doubleday.

Lebon, R.L. (1999). The Professional Vocalist: A Handbook for Commercial Singers and Teachers. Lanham, MD, Scarecrow Press.

Lewis, T.M. (1996). The Monkey-Rope, A Psychotherapist's Reflections on Relationships. New York, Bernel Books, Brunner/Mazel Inc.

Matheopoulos, H. (1991). Diva: Great Sopranos and Mezzos Discuss Their Art. London: V. Gollancz.

Matheopoulos, H. (1998). Diva: The New Generation: The Sopranos and Mezzos of the Decade Discuss Their Roles. Boston, MA, Northeastern University Press.

Papolos, J. (1984). The Performing Artist's Handbook. Cincinnati, OH, Writer's Digest Books.

Roussel, J.J. (1997). Simionato, How Cinderella Became Queen. Dallas, TX, Baskerville Publishers, Inc.

Ware, C. (1997). What's A Singing Competition All About? Journal of Singing, Sept/Oct, 3-6.

Character Portrayal

Balk, W. (1985). Performing Power: A New Approach for the Singer-Actor. Minneapolis, University of Minnesota Press.

Balk, W. (1991). The Radiant Performer, The Spiral Path to Performing Power. Minneapolis, University of Minneapolis Press.

Bollas, C. (1992). Being a Character: Psychoanalysis and Self Experience. New York, Hill and Wang.

Bollas, C. (1995). Cracking UP: The Work of Unconscious Experience. New York, Hill and Wang.

Landy, R.T. (1993). Persona and Performance, The Meaning of Role in Drama, Therapy, and Everyday Life. New York, Guilford Press.

Pisk, L. (1975). The Actor and His Body. New York, Theatre Arts Book.

Sabatine, J. (1983). The Actor's Image; Movement Training for Stage and Screen. New Jersey, Prentice Hall.

Stanislavsky, K. (1961). Stanislavsky on the Art of the Stage. (1st American ed.). New York, Hill and Wang.

Stanislavsky, K. & Rumyantsev, P. (1998). Stanislavsky on Opera. (E.R. Hapgood, trans.). London, Routledge.

Creativity

Coan, R.W. (1977). Hero, Artist, Sage or Saint? A Survey of Views on What is Variously Called Mental Health, Normality, Maturity, Self-actualization, and Human Fulfillment. New York, Columbia University Press.

Csikszentmihalyi, M. & Nakamura, J. (1984). The Dynamics of Intrinsic Motivation: A Study of Adolescents. In R.Ames & C.Ames (eds.) Research on Motivation in Education. (Vol.3, 45-71). Orlando, Academic Press.

Csikszentmihalyi, M. (1991). Flow: The Psychology of Optimal Experience. New York, Harper Perennial.

Csikszentmihalyi, M., Rathunde, K.R., & Whalen, S. (1993).

Talented Teenagers: The Roots of Success and Failure. Cambridge, England, Cambridge University Press.

Csikszentmihalyi, M. (1996). Creativity: Flow and the Psychology of Discovery and Invention. New York, Harper Collins.

Eigen, M. & Phillips, A. (1993). The Electrified Tightrope. Northvale, NJ, Jason Aronson.

Gardner, H. (1982). Art, Mind, and Brain, A Cognitive Approach to Creativity. New York, Basic Books.

Gardner, H. (1993). Creating Minds, An Anatomy of Creativity. New York, Basic Books.

Gedo, J.E. (1996). The Artist and His Emotional World: Creativity and Personality. New York, Columbia University Press.

Goleman, D., Kaufman, P., & Ray, M.L. (1992). The Creative Spirit. New York, Plume.

Miller, R. (1992). The Practicality of Creativity. The NATS Journal, Nov/Dec, 15-17.

Perkins, D.N., (1981). The Mind's Best Work. Cambridge, MA, Harvard University Press.

Reber, A.S. (1993). Implicit Learning and Tacit Knowledge, An Essay on the Cognitive Unconscious. New York, Oxford University Press.

Rosenbaum, M. (1990). Learned Resourcefulness, on Coping Skills, Self-Control, and Adaptive Behavior. New York, Springer Publishing Co.

Sawyer, R.K. (1998). Creativity in Performance. Greenwood Publishing Group.

Wyndham, T. (1998). Composition, Performance, Reception: Studies in the creative process in music. Ashgate Publishing Co.

Early Musical Development, Play

Bamberger, J.S. (1995). Mind Behind the Musical Ear: How Children Develop Musical Intelligence. Cambridge, MA, Harvard University Press.

Cohen, D. (1987). The Development of Play. London, Croom Helm.

Davies, C. (1992). Listen To My Song: A Study of Songs Invented by Children Aged 5-7 Years. British Journal of Music Education, 9(1), 19-48.

Deliège, I. & Sloboda, J.A. (1996). Musical Beginnings: Origins and Development of Musical Competence. New York, Oxford University Press.

Freeman, J. (1991). Gifted Children Growing Up. London, Heineman Educational.

Garvey, C. (1977). Play. Cambridge, MA, Harvard University Press.

Kagan, J. & Zentner, M.R. (1996). Perception of Music by Infants. Nature, 383,5.

Manturzewska, M. (1990). A Biographical Study of the Life-Span Development of Professional Musicians. Psychology of Music, 18, 112-139.

Michel, P. (1973). The Optimum Development of Musical Abilities In the First Years of Life. Psychology of Music, 1(2), 14-20.

Miller, P.H. (1983). Theories of Developmental Psychology. San Francisco, W.H. Freeman.

Mota, G. (1994). Music Development in the Early School Years: The Role of Aptitude, Music Instruction and Family Background. European Society for the Cognitive Sciences of Music Newsletter, April (5), 26-31.

Peery, J.C., Peery, I.W. & Draper, T. (1987). Music and Child Development. New York, Springer-Verlag.

Piaget, J. (1962). Play, Dreams, and Imitation in Childhood, New York, Norton.

Piaget, J. (1970). The Child's Conception of Time. New York, Basic Books.

Pruett, K.D. (1987). A Longtitudinal View of the Musical Gifts: Clinical Studies of the Blessings and Curses of Precocious Talents. Medical Problems of Performing Artists, March, 31-38.

Pruett, K.D. (1991). Psychological Aspects of the Development of Exceptional Young Performers and Prodigies. In R.T. Sataloff, A Brandfonbrener, & R.L. Lederman (eds.), Textbook of Performing Arts Medicine (pp.309-322). St. Louis, MO, MMB Music.

Winnicott, D.W. (1965). The Family and Individual Development. New York, Basic Books.

Winnicott, D.W. (1965). The Maturation Processes and the Facilitating Environment Studies in the Theory of Emotional Development. New York, International Universities Press.

Wright, K. (1991). Vision and Separation: Between Mother and Baby. Northvale, NJ, Jacob Aronson.

Emotion

Coleman, R.F. & Williams, R. (1978). Identification of Emotional States Using Perceptual and Acoustic Analysis. Transcripts of the Eighth Symposium on Care of the Professional Voice, Part I, 78-83. Philadelphia, The Voice Foundation.

Coleman, R.F. (1983). Single and Combined Attributes of Emotion. Transcripts of the 12th Symposium Care of the Professional Voice, Part I, 46-51. Philadelphia, The Voice Foundation.

Edwin, R. (1996). Attitude as Vocal Technique. The NATS Journal, Jan/Feb, 53-56.

Fonagy, I. (1981). Emotion, Voice and Music. Research Aspects on Singing, 33, 51-79. Royal Swedish Academy of Music.

Gfeller, K., Asmus, E., & Eckert, M. (1991). An Investigation of Emotional Response to Music and Text. Society for Research in Psychology of Music and Music Education, 19(2).

Goleman, D. (1995). Emotional Intelligence. New York, Bantam Books.

Kivy, P. (1989). Sound Sentiment: An Essay on the Musical Emotions, including the complete text of The Corded Shell. Philadelphia, Temple University Press.

Kratus, J. (1993). A Developmental Study of Children's Interpretation of Emotion in Music. Psychology of Music, 21, 3-19.

Meyer, L.B. (1956). Emotion and Meaning in Music. Chicago, University of Chicago Press.

Miller, L. (1989). To Beat Stress, Don't Relax, Get Tough. Psychology Today, Dec. 62-64.

Miller, R. (2001). Learning to Portray Emotion. Journal of Singing, May/June, 31-32.

Nielzen, S. & Zvonimir, N. (1982). Emotional Experience of Music as a Function of Musical Structure. Psychology of Music, 10(2), 7-17.

Oatley, K. (1992). Best Laid Schemes: The Psychology of Emotions. Cambridge, Cambridge University Press.

Provine, R. (2000). The Science of Laughter. Psychology Today, Nov/Dec, 58-61.

Stratton, V. & Zalanowski, A. (1991). The Effects of Music and Cognition on Mood. Journal of the Society for Research in Psychology of Music and Music Education, 19(2).

Torwogt, M. & Grinsven, F.W. (1991). Musical Expression of Moodstates. Journal of the Society for Research in Psychology of Music and Music Education, 19(2).

Vennard, W. (1911). Singers and Their Emotions. The American Music Teacher, April, 24-26.

Wickberg, D. (1998). The Senses of Humor: Self and Laughter in Modern America. Cornell University Press.

Gender

Barnett, R.C., Biener, L., & Baruch, G.K. (1987). Gender and Stress. New York, MacMillan Inc., Free Press.

Beall, A.E. & Sternberg, R.J. (1993). The Psychology of Gender. New York, Guilford Press.

Bern, S.L. (1981). One Consequence of Psychological Androgyny. Journal of Personality and Social Psychology, 31(634-643).

Bernstein, D. (1993). Female Identity Conflict in Clinical Practice. New Jersey, Jason Aronson.

Hudson, L. & Jacob, B. (1991). The Way Men Think. Yale University Press.

Koza, J.E. (1993-94). Big Boys Don't Cry (or Sing): Gender, Misogyny, and Homophobia in College Choral Methods Texts. The Quarterly Journal of Music Teaching and Learning, 4(4), 5(2), 48-64.

Miller, R. (1981). Male and Female Created He Them. The NATS Bulletin, Mar/Apr,43.

Interpretation

Bean, M. (1997). Bringing a Song to Life. Journal of Singing 53(1), 37-39, 53(2), 39-42.

Bernac, P. (1976). The Interpretation of French Song. New York, Norton.

Davies S. (1994). Musical Meaning and Expression. Ithaca, NY Cornell University Press.

Lehman, L. (1985). More Than Singing: The Interpretation of Songs. (Frances Walden, trans.). New York, Dover Publishers.

Stein, D.J. & Spilman, R. (1996). Poetry Into Song: Performance and Analysis of Lieder. New York, Oxford University Press.

Memorizing

Davis, R. (1994). Memorization for the Young Singer. The NATS Journal, Sept/Oct. 4-11,72.

Jones, M.R. (1976). Time, Our Last Dimension: Toward a New Theory of Perception, Attention, and Memory. Psychological Review, 83, 323-355.

Miller, G.A. (1956). The Magical Number Seven, Plus or Minus Two: Some Limits of Our Capacity for Processing Information. Psychology Review, 63(81-97).

Rose, S.P.R. (1992). The Making of Memory: From Molecules to Mind. New York, Anchor Books.

Motivation

Asmus, E.P. & Harrison, C.S. (1990). Characteristics of Motivation for Music, and Musical Aptitude of Undergrad Nonmusic Majors. Journal of Research in Music Education, 38(258-269)

Butt, D.C. (1987). Psychology of Sport: Behavior, Motivation, Personality, Performance. New York, Van Nostrand Reinhold Co.

Cattell, R.B. & Kline, P. (1977). The Scientific Analysis of Personality and Motivation. New York, Academic Press.

Lawrence, V. (1984). Will Knowing How My Voice Works Make Me Sing Better? The NATS Bulletin, Mar/Apr, 24-25.

Music and Psychology

Aiello, R., & Sloboda, J.A. (1994). Musical Perceptions. New York, Oxford University Press.

Bachman, J.L. (1991). Dalcroze Today: An Education Through and Into Music. (D.Parlett, trans.). Oxford, Clarendon Press.

Blacking, J. (1983). How Musical is Man? University of Washington Press.

Buck, P.C. (1987). Psychology for Musicians. Oxford, Oxford University Press.

Bunch, M. (1993). Dynamics of the Singing Voice. (2nd rev.ed.). Wien, New York, Springer-Verlag.

Cox, G.H. (1994). Applying "Inner Game" Strategies to the Art of Singing. The NATS Journal, Nov/Dec, 13/16.

Davies, J.B. (1978) The Psychology of Music. Stanford, CA. Stanford University Press.

Deutsch, D. (1982). The Psychology of Music. New York, Academic Press.

Duke, J. (1984). The Nature and Significance of Song. The NATS Bulletin, Jan/Feb, 19/22.

Edwin, R. (1989). The Bach to Rock Connection: Is Your Cerebellum Working? The NATS Journal, March/April, 38,50.

Gordon, E.E. (1998). Introduction to Research and The Psychology of Music. Chicago, GIA Publications.

Green, B. (1988). Gaining Control by Letting Go: The Inner Game of Music. The American Music Teacher, Jan, 12-15.

Günter, H. (1992). Mental Concepts in Singing, Psychological Approach, Part I. The NATS Journal, 48(5), May/June, 8.

Günter, H. (1992). Mental Concepts in Singing: Part II. The NATS Journal, Sept/Oct. 4-7.

Hargreaves, D. (1986). The Developmental Psychology of Music. Cambridge, Cambridge University Press.

Jones, M.R, & Holleran, S. (1992). Cognitive Bases of Musical Communication. Washington, DC, American Psychological Association.

Krumhansl, C.L. (1990). Cognitive Foundations of Musical Pitch. Oxford, Oxford University Press.

Lerdahl, F. & Jackendoff, R.S. (1983). A Generative Theory of Tonal Music. Cambridge, MA, MIT Press.

Maconie, R. (1990). The Concept of Music. New York, Oxford University Press.

Maconie, R. (1997). The Science of Music. New York, Oxford University Press.

Radocy, R.E. & Boyle, J.D. (1988). Psychological Foundations of Musical Behavior (2nd ed.) Springfield, IL, Charles C. Thomas.

Reid, C. (1975). Voice: Psyche and Soma. New York, Joseph Patelson.

Repp, B.H., (1993). Music as Motion: A Synopsis of Alexander Truslit's (1938) Gestaltung Und Bewegung in der Musik. Psychology of Music, 21, 48-72.

Rosen, C.R. & Sataloff, R.T. (1998). Psychological Considerations in Singers. In R.T. Sataloff, A.G. Brandfonbrener, & R.J.

Lederman (eds.), Performing Arts Medicine (2nd ed.). San Diego, CA, Singular Publishing Co.

Seashore, C.E. (1967). The Psychology of Music, (original edition 1938). New York, Dover.

Serafine, M.L. (1988). Music as Cognition: The Development of Thought in Sound. New York, Columbia University Press.

Shelton, L. (1997). Vocal Problem or Body Block? A Look at the Psyche of the Singer. Journal of Singing, May/June, 9-13,16-18.

Sloboda, J. (1985). The Musical Mind: The Cognitive Psychology of Music. Oxford, Oxford University Press.

Sloboda, J. (1988). Generative Processes in Music: The Psychology of Performance, Improvisation, and Composition. Oxford, Oxford University Press.

Sloboda, J. (1991). Music Structure and Emotional Response. Journal of the Society for Research in Psychology of Music and Music Education, 19(2).

Sloboda, J. (1993) Music Ability. In G.Bock, & K.Ackrill (eds.), The Origins and Development of High Ability, (pp. 187-199). Chichester, England, New York, Wiley.

Wallin, N.L., Merker, B., & Brown, S. (2000). The Origins of Music. Cambridge, MA, MIT Press.

Wormhoudt, P. (1982). An Overview of the Psychology of Singing and Teaching of Singing. Proceedings of the International Decade of Research in Singing, Rotterdam, June, 183-191.

Wormhoudt, P. (1984). Some Thoughts on the Psychology of Singing and Teaching Singing. The NATS Bulletin, May/June, 28-31.

Wormhoudt, P. (1986). A Framework for a Psychology of Singing and Teaching Singing. Journal of Research in Singing, May 45-48.

Wormhoudt, P. (1987). Facets of Psychology in the Development of a Singer. Proceedings of the International Conference on the Cognitive Psychology of Music, Liège, Belgium, University of Liège, June, 18-22.

Wormhoudt, P. (1991). On the Psychology of Singing and Teaching Singing. Proceedings of the 2nd International Congress of Voice Teachers, Philadelphia, PA, July, 21-24.

Performance

Dunsby, J. (1995). Performing Music: Shared Concerns. Oxford, Oxford University Press.

Emmons, S. & Sonntag, S. (1979). The Art of the Song Recital. New York, Schirmer.

Emmons, S. & Thomas, A. (1998). Power Performance for Singers: Transcending the Barriers. New York, Oxford University Press.

Hampton, M.E, (1991). The Voice in Performance Technique: Leading the Ear of the Audience. The NATS Journal, Nov/Dec, 6-9.

Helfgot, D. & Beeman, W.O. (1993). The Third Line: The Opera Performer as Interpreter. New York, Shirmer.

Miller, R. (1996). On the Art of Singing. New York, Oxford University Press.

Miller, R. (1997). Performance Thinking. The NATS Journal of Singing, Nov/Dec, 31-32.

Oswald, P. & Avery, M. (1998). Psychiatric Problems in Performing Artists. In R.T.Sataloff, A.G.Brandfonbrener, & R.J. Jederman (eds.), Performing Arts Medicine (2nd ed.). San Diego, CA. Singular Publishing Co.

Schenker, R. & Esser, H. (2000). The Art of Performance. New York, Oxford University Press.

Schneiderman, B. (1991). Confident Music Performance: The Art of Preparing. St. Louis, MO, MMB Music.

Stanislavsky, K. (1961). Stanislavsky on the Art of the Stage. New York, Hill and Wang.

Thom, P. (1993). For An Audience: A Philosophy of the Performing Arts. Philadelphia, Temple University Press.

Thompson, W., Sundberg, J., Friberg, A., & Fryden, L. (1989). The Use of Rules for Expression in the Performance of Melodies. Psychology of Music, 17(1), 63-82.

Performance Anxiety and Perfectionism

Aaron, S. (1986). Stage Fright, Its Role in Acting. Chicago, University of Chicago Press.

Antony, M. & Swinson, E. (1998). When Perfect Isn't Good Enough. Oakland, CA, New Harbinger Publications.

Caire, J.B. (1977). Understanding and Treating Performance Anxiety From a Cognitive Behavior Therapy Perspective. The NATS Journal, March/April, 27-30,51.

Gray, J.A. (1982). The Neuropsychology of Anxiety. New York, Oxford University Press.

Hanley,M.A. (1984). Creative Visualization: Antidote to Performance Anxiety. American Music Teacher, June, 28-29.

Keaton, A.L. (1981). Tuning Anxiety to Appropriate Levels. Transcripts of the 10th Symposium, Care of the Professional Voice, Part I. Philadelphia, The Voice Foundation.

Lazarus, A.L. (1984). In the Mind's Eye, the Power of Imagery for Personal Enrichment. New York, Guilford Press.

Nagel, J., Himle, D., & Papsdorf, J. (1981). Coping with Performance Anxiety. The NATS Journal, Mar/April, 26-27, 31-33.

Nagle, J. (1988). In Pursuit of Perfection: Career Choice and Performance Anxiety in Musicians. Medical Problems of Performing Artists, Dec, 140-145.

Nagel, J., Himle, D., & Papsdorf, J. (1989). Cognitive-Behavioral Treatment of Musical Performance Anxiety. Psychology of Music, 17(1), 12-21.

Ristad, E. (1982). A Soprano on Her Head: Right-side-up Reflections on Life and Other Performances. Moab, Utah, Real People Press.

Sataloff, R.T., Rosen, D.C., & Levy, S. (2000). Performance Anxiety: What Singing Teachers Should Know. Journal of Singing, 56(5), 33-40.

Steptoe, A. (1989). Stress, Coping, and Stage Fright in Professional Musicians. Psychology of Music, 17(1), 3-11.

Stollak, G. & Stollak, M.A. (1988). Psychological Contributions in Understanding and Alleviating Stage Fright. The NATS Journal, May/June, 10-12, 34.

Personality

Aronoff, J., Rabin, A.I., Zucker, R. (1987). The Emergence of Personality. New York, Springer Publishing Co. Costa, P.T. Jr., & Crae, M. (1992). Four Ways Five Factors Are Basic. Personality and Individual Difference, 13, 653-665.

Dews, C.L., Williams, M.S. (1989). Student Musicians' Personality, Styles, Stresses, and Coping Patterns. Psychology of Music, 17(1), 10-14.

Kemp, A. (1994). Aspects of Upbringing as Revealed in the Personalities of Musicians. University of Northern Colorado, The Quarterly Journal of Music Teaching and Learning, 5(4), 34-41.

Kemp, A. (1996). The Musical Temperament: Psychology and Personality in Musicians. New York, Oxford University Press.

Maslow, A.H. & Frager, R. (1987). Motivation and Personality, (3rd ed.). New York, Harper and Row.

Miller, R. (1998). The Reluctant Student. The NATS Journal, Jan/Feb, 41-42.

Schleuter, S.L. (1971). An Investigation of the Interrelation of Personality Traits, Music Aptitude and Musical Achievement. Studies in the Psychology of Music, Vol.8. Iowa City, IA, University of Iowa Press.

Wubbenhorst, T.M. (1994). Personality Characteristics of Music Education and Performers. Psychology of Music, 22, 63-74.

Psycholinguistics

Ellis, A. & Beattie, G. (1992). The Psychology of Language and Communication. East Sussex, England, Lawrence Erlbaum Assoc,Ltd.

Thass-Thienemann, T. (1973). The Interpretation of Language. New York, Jacob Aronson.

Wormhoudt, A. (1982). Introduction to Diwan al Mutanabbi, Translation and Commentary. Oskaloosa, IA, William Penn College.

Self

Haskell, J.A. (1987). Vocal Self-Perception: The Other Side of the Equation. Journal of Voice, 1(2), 172-179. Philadelphia, The Voice Foundation.

Kelso, J.A.S. (1995). Dynamic Patterns: The Self-Organization of Brain and Behavior. Cambridge, MA, MIT Press.

Kleinke, C.L. (1978). Self-Perception, the Psychology of Personal Awareness. San Francisco, CA, W.H. Freeman & Co.

Krueger, D.W. (1989). Body Self and Psychological Self. New York, Brunner/Mazel, Inc.

Lichtenstein, M. (1977). The Dilemma of Human Identity. New Jersey, Jacob Aronson.

Lipson, A. & Perkins, W.N. (1990). BLOCK—Getting Out of Your Own Way. New York, Carol Pulishing Group.

McKay, M. & Fanning, P. (1992). Self-Esteem, A Proven Program for Assessing, Improving, and Maintaining Your Self-Esteem. Oakland, CA, New Harbinger Publications Inc.

Mruk, C.J. (1995). Self-Esteem Research, Theory, and Practice. New York, Springer Publishing Co.

Rosen, C., Sataloff, R, Evans, H. & Hawkshaw, M. (1983). Self-Esteem and Singers: Singing "Healthy", Singing "Hurt". The NATS Journal, March/April, 32-35.

Scharff, J.S. (1994). The Autonomous Self, The Work of John D.

Sutherland. New Jersey, Jacob Aronson.

Truchses, D.D. (1989, rev.ed.). From Fear to Freedom, Choosing High Self-Esteem. Golden, CO, Fulcrum Inc.

Vispoel, W.P. (1995). Integrating Self-Perception of Musical Skill Into Contemporary Models of Self-Concept. Quarterly Journal of Music Teaching and Learning, 5(4), 42-59. University of Northern Colorado.

Senses, Hearing

Ackerman, D. (1991). A Natural History of the Senses. New York, Random House.

Campbell, D.G. (1989). The Roar of Silence, Healing Powers of Breath, Tone and Music. Wheaton, IL, The Theosophical Publishing House.

Carr, D.E. (1972). The Forgotten Senses. Garden City, NY, Doubleday.

Madaule, P. (1994). When Listening Comes Alive, A Guide to Effective Learning and Communication. Norval, Ontario, Moulin Publishers.

Madaule, P. (2001). Listening and Singing. Journal of Singing, May/June, 15-20.

McAdams, S. & Bigand, E. (1993). Thinking in Sound: The Cognitive Psychology of Human Audition. Oxford, Oxford University Press.

Sundberg, J. (1981). To Perceive One's Own Voice and Another Person's Voice. Research Aspects of Singing, 33.

Sundberg, J. (1982). Perception of Singing. In D.Deutch (ed.). The Psychology of Music, 59-98. New York, Academic Press.

Tomatis, A. (1991). The Conscious Ear. Barrytown, Station Hill Press.

Tomatis, A. (1996). The Ear and Language. Norval, Ontario, Moulin Publishing.

Stress

Barnett, R, Biener, L, Baruch, G. (1987). Gender and Stress. New York, MacMillan.

Bavender, P.E. (1986). Winners and Losers: The Dynamics of Competition. The NATS Bulletin, Sept/Oct. 18-20.

Davis, M., Robbins, E., & McKay, M. (1992). The Relaxation and Stress Reduction Workbook (4th ed.). Oakland, CA, New Harbinger Publications, Inc.

DeNelsky, G.V. (1985). Stress of the Performing Arts: A Special Psychotherapeutic Challenge. Aspen, CO, Proceedings of the Third Annual Symposium on Medical Problems of Musicians, July, 66-67.

Grindea, C. (1982). Tensions in the Performance of Music. New York, Alexander Broude Inc.

Kabat-Zinn, J. (1990). Full Catastrophe Living: Using the Wisdom of Your Body and Mind to Face Stress, Pain, and Illness. New York, Delacorte, Random House.

Lawrence, V. (1986). Stress in Singers. The NATS Journal, Jan/Feb, 26-27, 50.

Lehrer, P.M. & Woolfolk, R.L. (1993). Principles and Practice of Stress Management (2nd ed.). New York, Guilford Press.

Ohrenstein, D. (1999). Physical Tension, Awareness Techniques, and Singing. Journal of Singing, Sept.Oct. 23-27.

Vocal Pedagogy

Blades-Zeller, E. (1994). Vocal Pedagogy in the United States: Interviews with Exemplary Teachers of Applied Voice. Journal of Research in Singing, June, 1-87.

Boardman, S.B. (1992). Vocal Training for a Career in Music Theater: A Pedagogy. The NATS Journal, Sept/Oct, 8-15, 47-48.

Brammer, L.H. & MacDonald, G. (1996). The Helping Relationship, Process and Skills (6th ed.). Boston, MA, Allyn & Bacon.

Brown, W.E. (1957). Vocal Wisdom, Maxims of Giovanni Battista Lamperti. Boston, Crescendo Publishing Co.

Cady, H.L. (1965). We Are Only Human, Interpersonal Relations in the Voice Studio. The NATS Bulletin, Sept/Oct, 16-20.

Doscher, B.M. (1988). The Functional Unity of the Singing Voice. Metuchen, NJ, Scarecrow Press.

Garcia, M. (1947). A Complete Treatise on the Art of Singing, Part One (D.V. Paschke, trans, 1983 ed.). New York, DaCapo Press.

Heirich, J.R. (1993). The Alexander Technique and Voice Pedagogy. The NATS Journal, 49(5), 16-18.

Sundberg, J. (1987). The Science of the Singing Voice. DeKalb, IL, Northern Illinois University Press.

Thurman, L. & Welch, G. (2000). Bodymind and Voice: Foundation of Voice Education, Rev.Ed. Iowa City, IA, National Center for Voice and Speech.

Titze, I.R. (1994). Principles of Voice Production. Englewood Cliffs, NJ, Prentice Hall.

Titze, I.R. (1995). What's in a Voice? New Scientist, 23 Sept,38-42.

Ware, C. (1998). Basics of Vocal Pedagogy: The Foundations and Process of Singing. Boston, McGraw-Hill.

Wormhoudt, P.S. (1981). Building the Voice as an Instrument. Oskaloosa, IA, William Penn College.

Yenne, V. (1992). No One Ever Told Me. The NATS Journal, 3, 44-45.

Voice

Boone, D.R. (1997). Is Your Voice Telling On You?: How to Find Out and Use Your Natural Voice (2nd ed.). San Diego, CA, Singular Publishing Group.

Brodnitz, F.S. (1979). Psychological Considerations in Voice

Therapy. Transcripts of the Eighth Symposium, Care of the Professional Voice, Part III, 40-45.

Brown, O. (1999). Discover Your Voice. San Diego, CA, Singular Publishing Group.

Linklater, K. (1976). Freeing the Natural Voice. New York, Drama Books.

Rosen, C. & Sataloff, R.T. (1997). Psychology of Voice Disorders. San Diego, CA, Singular Publishing Group.

Sataloff, R.T. (1992). The Human Voice. Scientific American, Dec. 108-115.

Shelton, L. (1997). Vocal Problem or Body Block? A Look at the Psyche of the Singer. Journal of Singing, May/June, 9-18.

Titze, I. (1995) What's In A Voice? New Scientist, 12 Sept, 38-42.

Welch, G. (1994). The Assessment of Singing. Journal of the Society for Research in Psychology of Music and Music Education, 22(1), 3-19.

INDEX

Get Published, Inc!
Thorofare, NJ 08086
15 October 2009
BA2009288